Snodgrass Hill
Walking Tour Map

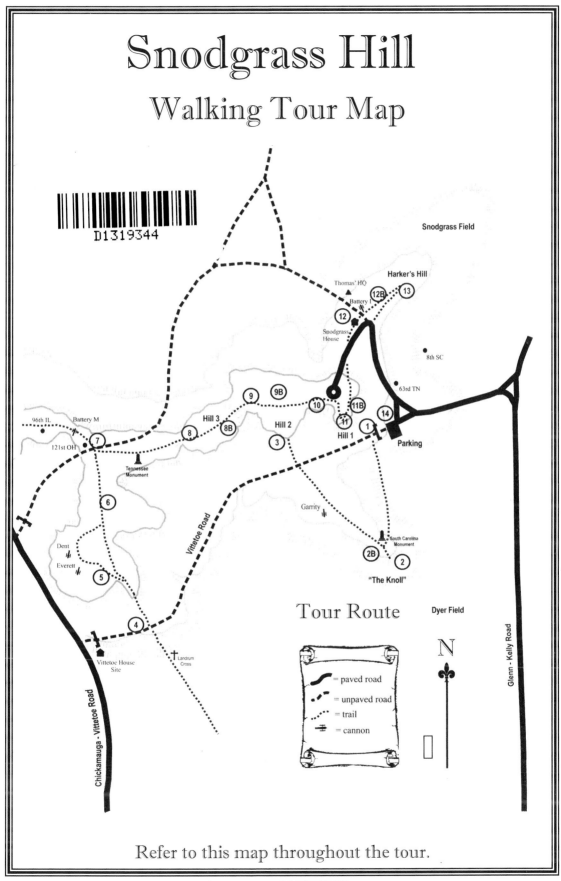

D1319344

Snodgrass Field

Harker's Hill

Thomas' HQ

Battery

12B 13

12

Snodgrass House

8th SC

63rd TN

9 9B

10 11B

96th IL   Battery M

Hill 3

Hill 2

8 8B

3

11

14

Hill 1

1

Parking

7

121st OH

Tennessee Monument

6

Garrity

South Carolina Monument

Vittetoe Road

Dent

Everett

2B

2

5

"The Knoll"

Dyer Field

Tour Route

4

Vittetoe House Site

Landrum Cross

Chickamauga - Vittetoe Road

Glenn - Kelly Road

= paved road
= unpaved road
= trail
= cannon

N

Refer to this map throughout the tour.

THE BATTLE OF CHICKAMAUGA

THE

FIGHT FOR SNODGRASS HILL

AND THE

ROCK OF CHICKAMAUGA

A HISTORY AND WALKING TOUR

By:

ROBERT L. CARTER

MAPS BY JAMES A. BOYD

PUBLISHED BY

MELICA BOOKS, LLC

155 CAMP LANE
CARROLLTON, GEORGIA 30117

WWW.MELICABOOKS.COM

Cover Picture
"Rock of Chickamauga" by Dale Gallon. Courtesy of Gallon Historical Art www.gallon.com

ISBN 978-0-9835495-3-6

Map design & creation: James A. Boyd
Printer liaison & publishing advisor: Bev Bruemmer Books
Book layout & cover design: A. D. Pickle

This book is lovingly dedicated

to my daughters,

Melanie and Jessica

INTRODUCTION

The Battle of Chickamauga, September 19-20, 1863, remains one of the most confusing and least understood battles of the Civil War. In the deep woods and on the small farms of this remote northwest Georgia locale, a fierce battle raged that ranks second only to Gettysburg in the number of losses incurred. Union Major General William S. Rosecrans' Army of the Cumberland and Confederate General Braxton Bragg's Army of Tennessee grappled for two days of bloody, indecisive fighting before a Federal mistake and a fortunately-timed Southern attack changed the fortunes of the battle. Like many Civil War battlefields, this area was poor and insignificant until 37,000 American casualties made it hallowed ground.

More than 350,000 people visit Chickamauga National Military Battlefield each year, but very few take the time to park their cars and walk a portion of it. The Battle of Chickamauga makes an interesting study, and the fight for Snodgrass Hill (some call it Horseshoe Ridge) was a pivotal and dramatic portion of that fight. As the casualty lists attest, both sides, North *and* South, fought with a determined bravery not exceeded on any battlefield of the Civil War. The Confederates' many determined assaults on the hill, and the Federals' tenacious defense, sometimes without ammunition and at the point of the bayonet, are, sadly, largely forgotten today. Also forgotten are the individual stories of the officers and men who fought here. This book is written in an effort to preserve those memories.

By walking the field, you gain a unique appreciation for the difficult fight for Snodgrass Hill. You experience the steepness of the topography, the ravines, and the curving nature of the hill crests, all of which greatly aided the Federal units in their defense of Horseshoe Ridge and hurt the Confederates in their ability to organize their assaults. Walking this ground rewards you with a much deeper understanding of the ebb and flow of the attack and defense of Snodgrass Hill. Plus, it is a *beautiful* walk, and great exercise besides!

This is not a book only for Civil War experts. On the contrary, anyone even generally interested in the Civil War will enjoy the walking tour. This guidebook leads you to places of significance on the battlefield and describes some of the events that make that place noteworthy. For a detailed account of the battle you will need to refer to some of the books on the Suggested Reading List at the end.

The walk is approximately 2.2 miles in length and takes from 90 minutes to 2 hours to complete, making for a very nice morning or afternoon stroll. The total time of your walk will depend on your time at each stop, and how many monuments and tablets you pause to read along the way—and there are many! There are no restrooms on Snodgrass Hill, so be sure to avail yourselves of the facilities at the Chickamauga National Military Battlefield Park Headquarters before beginning. Even though the tour has been carefully designed so that climbing hills has been kept to a minimum, the walk can be arduous for some. The trail does have many rest stops, and you'll welcome having a water bottle.

You will be walking in the steps of thousands of brave men who displayed courage, tenacity, sacrifice, and toughness on the slopes and crests of Snodgrass Hill. The seven hours of desperate fighting on this ground ended in a decisive Confederate victory—and with an immortal sobriquet for a Union general born in Virginia: "The Rock of Chickamauga."

By Alfred R. Waud

Confederate Attack at Chickamauga

Table Of Contents

MAPS

ACKNOWLEDGMENTS

This book could not have been completed without the guidance and assistance of others. First, I would like to thank our Civil War study group, the Carroll County Irregulars, whose sponsorship made this book possible. From Chickamauga to Gettysburg, and everywhere in between, there are no better companions and battlefield trampers. Thanks to Dr. Jack Crews, Dr. Lawrence Alligood (who had the inspiration at our dinner in Fredericksburg, Virginia), Dr. Dean Talley, Dr. Charlie Hubbard, Mr. Loy Howard, Dr. Peter Worthy, Dr. Tom Fitzgerald, Dr. Bill Watson, Dr. Jeff Lindsey, and their wonderful wives. There are no finer people anywhere than the Irregulars.

For walking the tour route with me, reading the manuscript, editing, and making many valuable suggestions, I give special thanks to Dr. Tom Carter, my brother, and associate professor of English and communication at Roanoke College in Salem, Virginia. My wife, Georgia, reviewed the book at every stage and helped immensely. I appreciate your help and advice more than you know.

A book of this type needs excellent maps, and I lucked into one of the best. Jim Boyd spent untold hours making complicated terrain simple and readable. He is that rare combination of technician and artist. My book is richer for his contribution. Thank you, Jim.

All roads leading to the serious study of the Battle of Chickamauga go through Jim Ogden, historian at Chickamauga and Chattanooga National Military Park. His knowledge of the battle is encyclopedic, and he shares this knowledge unselfishly and with clarity. Many thanks to Jim for answering my numerous questions, leading me to sources, and taking the time out of his busy schedule to walk across Horseshoe Ridge with me. Lee White, also of Chickamauga and Chattanooga National Park, gave me insight into different aspects of the fight for Horseshoe Ridge. Always eager to discuss the battle, he read the first part of the manuscript, offering clarification on many points.

Peter Worthy, Jim Meredith, and the late Jim Swisher are three people whose love of walking the old battlefields matches my own. I have especially enjoyed those trips that have been off the beaten path. I thank you for the years of conversation, study, map-reading, arguing, and fun. We have learned tremendously on all of our many trips together.

Beverly Bruemmer, Amber Pickle, and Thomas Cook all have my gratitude for designing, formatting, and editing this book. In addition, thanks go to Scott Tidmore for assisting with the photographs.

And, lastly, my gratitude to all of you who keep alive the memory of those who gave "the last full measure of devotion."

Robert Carter
November 17, 2011
Carrollton, Georgia

The Carroll County Irregulars on tour.
Lookout Mountain, 2011.

OVERVIEW
THE MARCH TO SNODGRASS HILL

The summer of 1863 witnessed one of the most brilliant campaigns of the Civil War. Beginning on June 23 from Murfreesboro, Tennessee, the commander of the Army of Cumberland, Union Major General William S. Rosecrans had maneuvered Confederate General Braxton Bragg's Army of Tennessee south of Chattanooga without fighting a major battle. With less than 50,000 men to Rosecrans' 80,000, Bragg had to execute a series of retreats in the face of constant feints and flanking movements. On June 24 Rosecrans' Army of the Cumberland quickly poured through Liberty and Hoover's Gaps, capturing Manchester and Shelbyville on the Duck River on June 27. Bragg's plan was to fight at Tullahoma, but the Federals again outflanked Bragg's right, and on June 30 Bragg ordered a retreat across the Elk

Major General
William S. Rosecrans,
USA

River to the vicinity of Winchester. Once again perceiving a flanking movement, on July 2 Bragg ordered the Army of Tennessee all the way back to Chattanooga. Rosecrans then paused to stockpile supplies for his move to take Chattanooga.

General
Braxton Bragg, CSA

Rosecrans' plan this time was to feint to Bragg's right flank and then cross the Tennessee River to the south of Chattanooga at Shellmound, Bridgeport, and Stevenson. On August 29 full-scale crossings of the Tennessee River began. The Army of Tennessee, once again being out-maneuvered, had to abandon Chattanooga. By September 7 the van of the Southern army, a victim of numerical disadvantage and aggressive flanking maneuvers, was in motion south to LaFayette, Georgia. On the 8th, Chattanooga officially fell to the Federals with scarcely a shot being fired.

But success bred danger. Militarily, Chattanooga was the geographic and logistical key to Atlanta and the Deep South. Rosecrans, elated that the goal of his campaign had been achieved much more easily than he anticipated, and being informed that Bragg's army was in full retreat, made plans to capture LaFayette and concentrate the three corps of his army. From LaFayette, Rosecrans could move either to the railroad at Dalton or south to Rome. But for now, the Army of the Cumberland lay scattered over 50 miles of rugged terrain, moving slowly through the gaps and passes of Lookout Mountain.

The vital piece of information that Rosecrans did not have was that Bragg had concentrated the Confederate army at LaFayette. He had stopped retreating and was looking for a fight. Bragg sent soldiers acting as deserters into the Union army with false information that the Army of Tennessee was in full flight and would not stop short of Atlanta. The ruse held some credence with the overconfident Rosecrans, leading him to disperse his three corps of infantry beyond supporting distance of one another. In addition, Bragg's army had received significant reinforcements, and more were on the way from Virginia. Bragg's plan was to attack the three Union corps in detail, beginning with Major General George H. Thomas' XIV Corps coming out of Stevens's Gap into McLemore's Cove, directly west of LaFayette.

Thomas, though, was rightfully cautious. He was not so sure that the Confederate Army was in such disarray and retreating so rapidly. Because of the widely separated Federal corps, he knew the situation was dangerous. When his Second Division, under the command of Major General James S. Negley, met stiffening Southern resistance west of Dug Gap on September 10, and Confederate prisoners told of Bragg's concentration at LaFayette, Thomas suspected a trap. He briefly reinforced Negley with two brigades from Brigadier General Absalom Baird's First Division before ordering their withdrawal on September 11. Thomas considered himself lucky to escape. He was also deeply concerned for the rest of the divided Army of the Cumberland.

Luck was not needed, however. In McLemore's Cove, Bragg's plan had miscarried due to a number of factors including miscommunication, caution, uncertainty, disobedience of orders, and subordinate commanders new to the Army of Tennessee who had never worked in concert before.

Bragg was enraged at the failure of his carefully planned strategy and his chance to destroy the Federal army one corps at a time.

Lee and Gordon's Mill.
A wartime view.

If Bragg was enraged, Rosecrans was now deeply concerned for the safety of his army. No longer overconfident, he ordered his three widely separated corps to concentrate at Lee and Gordon's Mill as rapidly as possible. If Bragg attacked before the Army of the Cumberland could be reunited, Rosecrans knew that disaster was a possibility. Major General Alexander McD. McCook's XX Corps and Thomas' XIV Corps slid north, while Major General Thomas L. Crittenden's XXI Corps moved south from Ringgold. To Rosecrans' immense relief, the concentration of his army was effected on September 17.

Rosecrans' relief was short-lived. With his army gathered in the Lee and Gordon's Mill area, Bragg deployed to the east of that point. New information placed a strong element of Confederates north, in Ringgold. Rosecrans knew that Chattanooga, his prize, lay in danger. Not only would it be impossible for the one brigade left there to hold against the whole Confederate army, but also Rosecrans had heard unsubstantiated rumors that Lt. General James Longstreet's Corps from General Robert E. Lee's Army of Northern Virginia had reinforced the Army of Tennessee. True or not, this information had to be considered. Although Rosecrans did not, or would not, believe this information to be true, he *did* believe reports of mounting Confederate pressure from his northern cavalry outpost commanders at Alexander's Bridge and Reed's Bridge.

Now that Longstreet was at hand, Bragg developed another plan. His strategy, to cross to the west side of Chickamauga Creek and move south to Lee and Gordon's Mill, would cut the Federal army off from Chattanooga and drive it back into McLemore's Cove. There, he could trap the Army of the Cumberland against the rugged face of Lookout Mountain and destroy it.

Lieutenant General James Longstreet, CSA

On September 18 Union Colonels Robert H. G. Minty's cavalry at Reed's Bridge and John T. Wilder's mounted infantry at Alexander's Bridge fought significant holding actions against the Confederate infantry. The pressure reached a critical point. That evening, Rosecrans ordered Thomas' XIV Corps to make an all night march north on the LaFayette Road to the Kelly farm. This rare night march changed the location of the Union left flank and possibly saved the Army of the Cumberland from destruction. The stage was now set for the opening of the Battle of Chickamauga.

Saturday, September 19, 1863
Day One

Thomas had no sooner arrived at the Kelly farm early September 19 than he received a report from his cavalry that a lone Confederate brigade stood west of Chickamauga Creek and could be easily gobbled up. Even though many of the Union soldiers had not had time to eat breakfast, Thomas ordered Brigadier General John M. Brannan's division to move forward immediately and capture the lone Confederate brigade. Brannan's three brigades of Col. John T. Croxton, Col. Ferdinand Van Derveer, and Col. John M. Connell moved east. With Croxton in the lead at 7:30 a.m., just to the west of Jay's Mill, they encountered Confederates, but not one lone brigade. The Confederates were there in force.

The morning's fight was a series of charges and counter-charges. Neither side could gain a clear picture of where the other was or what each was trying to do. Reinforcements arrived and were fed into the conflagration. The fight expanded quickly. In the deep woods, control by brigade commanders was difficult at best and almost impossible by division and corps commanders. The casualty rate grew alarmingly by the minute. Infantry units from both sides were in one moment victorious and charging ahead yet in the next were reeling from the enemy who appeared as if by magic on their flank or rear. Combat became furious, confusing, and frightening in the deep woods of Chickamauga. When it seemed that the storm had peaked, other units were added to the battle and the fury erupted anew. *(In a lull in the battle, the powder-stained Croxton sent a cryptic message back to corps commander Thomas asking just which of those five Confederate brigades he was to have captured. Thomas' response, if any, is lost to history.)*

By afternoon, forward elements from Longstreet's Corps entered the battle. Confederate Major General John Bell Hood moved forward on the south end of the battlefield at the Viniard farm. Hood attacked viciously and gained some initial success, but he met Union Col. John Wilder's Lightning Brigade of mounted infantry armed with Spencer seven-shot repeating rifles and was driven back. Bragg ordered Major General A. P. Stewart's division forward around the Brotherton farm. Stewart briefly pierced the Union line, but the blue infantry drove his brigades back across the LaFayette Road. Lastly on this sanguine day, Confederate Major General Patrick R. Cleburne's division attacked the Federal center at 7:30 p.m. in a rare night attack. After the noisy, confusing, and indecisive assault came to a close, the combat for the day ended. On this chilly autumn night, an eerie quiet settled over the battlefield, punctuated unnervingly by the moans and screams of hundreds—thousands—of wounded soldiers on both sides.

The frightening losses for the day, and the carnage on that Saturday, September 19, rank it as one of the three bloodiest days of the entire Civil War: September 17, 1862, at Antietam; July 2, 1863, at Gettysburg; and now September 19, 1863, at Chickamauga.

During the night, both armies aligned themselves roughly parallel with the LaFayette Road, the Union Army to the west of the road, and the Confederate Army to the east. Bragg ordered an attack of the Union left flank at first light ("day dawn") and reorganized his army into two wings before retiring for the night. Across the way, Rosecrans summoned a Council of War at his headquarters at the Widow Glenn's. Typically, his nervous energy kept him awake all night. Neither general planned to retreat.

Sunday, September 20, 1863
Day Two

The second day of the Battle of Chickamauga opened with . . . silence. Bragg's plan for an early morning attack on the Federal left flank had miscarried. Neither the Confederate corps commander on the right nor the division commander who was to lead the assault had received orders from headquarters telling them what to do. Bragg's orders never reached his unit commanders.

His patience at an end after waiting unsuccessfully for the sound of the guns which would signal the opening of the attack, Bragg rode quickly to his right flank to ascertain for himself the cause of the delay. Hearing all the reasons his orders were not followed and becoming exceedingly frustrated, he summarily bypassed his corps commanders and sent orders to attack directly to the division commanders. At 9:30 a.m., hours behind schedule, Maj. Gen. John C. Breckinridge's division on the far Southern right finally moved forward.

The delay proved a costly one for the Confederates and a godsend for Thomas' Federals on their battle line behind the Kelly house. Before dawn and without orders from senior commanders, the Union soldiers began to construct crude breastworks out of any material at hand: fence posts, logs, limbs, or large rocks. The men borrowed axes from the artillery units and felled trees to add to the breastwork. The blue troops worked quickly, and soon this protective breastwork stood two to three feet high. It was just high enough to give a soldier kneeling or firing prone good protection, and just high enough to hold against the furious assaults about to be unleashed against them by the Southerners.

Breckinridge's Confederate division hit the Union line first. His three brigades mauled Brig. Gen. John Beatty's Federal brigade to the north of Thomas' defenses, and for a time even fought to the rear of the Kelly house line. The attacks were all eventually beaten back with terrific loss. Of Breckinridge's three brigade commanders, Helm was killed and Adams was wounded and captured. Breckinridge was followed on his left by Cleburne's division. Cleburne's men fought bravely but were matched in valor by the blue soldiers fighting behind their breastworks. Ultimately, the Confederates were pushed back. Cleburne also lost one of his brigade commanders; Deshler was killed in the attack. Next, at about 10:30 a.m., A. P. Stewart's Southern division attacked on Cleburne's left. Like Breckinridge and Cleburne, Stewart also met the withering fire of the Federals behind their breastworks, and his attack likewise stalled.

From 9:30 a.m. until noon the attacks against the Federal left were strong and incessant. At times it seemed the Union line would be overwhelmed, but Thomas had the answer for each emergency. Rosecrans intended to reinforce his left with the whole Army of the Cumberland if necessary. Thomas was happy to oblige by continuously calling for reinforcements. Units were constantly in motion headed to the left, and finally, at about 11:00 a.m., Rosecrans ordered three brigades led by Brigadier General Thomas J. Wood out of line and moved to the left "to support Reynolds." Not only did Reynolds' division not need supporting, but the move left an enormous gap in the Federal line.

At just this time, by chance, Longstreet launched his attack. About 11:15 a.m., three Confederate divisions commanded by Bushrod Johnson, Evander Law, and Joseph Kershaw moved across the Brotherton farm and through the gap in the Union line almost without opposition. They rushed through the woods and burst into the Dyer field. In moments, the 11,000 Confederates in this column broke the Federal line, routed the right wing of the Army of the Cumberland, drove Rosecrans and two of his three corps commanders from the field, and threatened to destroy the whole Union army.

Only Gen. George Thomas and the high ground surrounding George Washington Snodgrass' tiny farm stood in the way of complete Southern victory.

Is it Called Snodgrass Hill or Horseshoe Ridge?
Terrain Features of the Battlefield

Visitors ask constantly, "Is it called Snodgrass Hill or Horseshoe Ridge?" The correct answer is — both. In some accounts it is called collectively "The Battle for Snodgrass Hill" and in others "The Battle for Horseshoe Ridge." At the time, the soldiers themselves didn't know exactly what to call all the features of this part of the battlefield, and they made note of the ridge using all sorts of names. Many contemporary accounts of the battle used the terms pretty much interchangeably, and the loose terminology will show up in some of the quotes I've used. In this book, I have tried to follow the lead of most modern accounts and distinguish between the two names.

"Snodgrass Hill" refers to the area around the Snodgrass house itself. The small, bare ridge running just northeast down the hill from the Snodgrass house is usually called the Snodgrass Spur or Harker's Hill (this being the ridge on which Harker rallied his men after his fight with Kershaw).

"Horseshoe Ridge," a name that really didn't get used until after the battle, refers to the series of summits and hollows that stretch to the south and west of the Snodgrass house. In fact, it is shaped nothing like a horseshoe. The ridge is a confusing series of hills, ravines and ridges, its crest curving in all directions but with a general orientation of east to west. For clarity in understanding the action here, these hills have become known as Hill 1, Hill 2, and Hill 3 (see the Walking Tour Map on page 1).

The view from the
Snodgrass Cabin to Hill 1

Hill 1 begins at the Snodgrass house and reaches its crest about 300 feet south.

The view from Hill 1
to Hill 2

Hill 2 lies west of Hill 1 about 400 feet and is higher in elevation.

The view from Hill 2 to Hill 3

Hill 3 is 300 feet west of Hill 2 and slightly higher in elevation. When walking the ground, it is not difficult to tell where each separate hill is because each holds a cluster of monuments.

If this all sounds confusing now, imagine how the soldiers felt in 1863. The individual soldiers in the ranks had little notion of where they were. Their officers often couldn't see their own troops or supporting units, much less the positions or movements of the enemy. The confounding series of hills and ravines, the curvature of the ridge crests, and the lack of visibility in the woods created a tactical nightmare for the Confederates trying to take Horseshoe Ridge. That is why so many soldiers who fought here thought this was the most frightening battle they participated in during the Civil War.

At the time of the battle the land looked much the same as it does today. The area around the Snodgrass buildings and to the north and northwest was clear of timber and used as fields for crops. In places around the fields, visibility was as much as 200 to 300 yards through the trees because of the lack of underbrush. It was a first-growth forest; plus, the farm animals ran free and ate the leaves as far up as they could reach. The hills themselves stood heavily wooded and covered in underbrush. The land here has been little disturbed since 1863.

Directions for the Tour

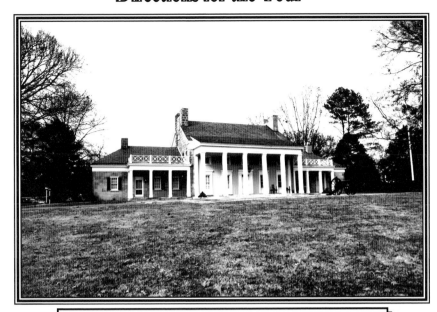

Visitor Center, Chickamauga National Military Park

Plan to visit the Visitor Center at Chickamauga National Battlefield Park before your tour. You will find the excellent park staff to be most helpful and informative. The museum and a film presentation will offer a wealth of background information on the Battle of Chickamauga. A fine bookstore offers a variety of accounts of the battle. The Visitor Center also houses the Fuller Gun Collection, which contains weapons of the same type as were used by both sides in the battle. Of special interest is the .56 cal. Colt 5-shot Revolving Rifle that was used to great effect by the 21st Ohio in their heroic stand on Horseshoe Ridge. Look for it in the second alcove on the left.

Note to those wishing to walk the tour: Make use of the Visitor Center restrooms before leaving. There are no restrooms on Snodgrass Hill.

GETTING THERE: Exit Park Headquarters. Turn <u>RIGHT</u> onto Highway 27 (Lafayette Road) heading south. Proceed 1.5 miles, and then turn <u>RIGHT</u> onto Dyer Road at the Brotherton House. Drive 0.2 miles, and then turn <u>RIGHT</u> at the stop sign onto Glenn-Kelly Road. Travel 0.6 miles and bear <u>LEFT</u> at the fork in the road (follow the Battlefield Tour sign). Then in 0.1 mile bear <u>LEFT</u> at the next fork in the road as you ascend Snodgrass Hill. Park on the left in the small parking area just in front of the bar that blocks the road. (Vittetoe Road is closed to vehicular traffic.) Exit your vehicle and walk to the back of it facing the hill in front of you.

STOP - 1

Snodgrass Hill

The steep slope of Snodgrass Hill

You are now looking at Snodgrass Hill with the same view that many Confederates had on the afternoon of September 20, 1863. The hill in front of you is known as Hill 1. It was the first place (sector) on the ridge that was occupied by the Federals. Union reinforcements fell in place both to the right and left of this point during the day, extending their defensive battle line ultimately to more than 1,200 yards. Some of these reinforcements were fragments of units that could be rallied after the breakthrough, some were brigades and regiments ordered to this spot, and some arrived unexpectedly. Southern commanders kept trying to flank this position, but on each occasion the Federals were able to extend their line just in time.

Note the steepness of the hill and the uneven curve of the crest. This greatly aided the Union troops on top as they were stationary and in line, but it impaired the Confederate regiments. The Southerners experienced difficulty maintaining their battle lines on the steep hillsides. Soldiers making repeated attacks uphill soon became exhausted. One Southern regimental commander said his men were "panting like dogs tired out in the chase." Sharp eyes can spot the Union monuments atop the hill.

Terrain always plays an important part in any battle, but at Chickamauga it was crucial in saving the Army of the Cumberland. Were it not for the fact that Thomas could improvise a line on high ground that ran east to west, perpendicular to his Kelly House line, Longstreet's infantry would have overrun the broken and panicked Federals before they could rally. He might have taken the four divisions that were deployed in an arc around the Kelly farm (Battleline Road) from the rear. Besides being a strong defensive position, Snodgrass Hill (Horseshoe Ridge) became a critical rallying point for the Federals. This high ground gave them the confidence to make a stand.

<u>Directions:</u> **Now turn to your left and walk around the bar-barrier that blocks vehicles from entering the Vittetoe Road. Walk 50 yards down the Vittetoe Road (this road was here at the time of the battle) and take the hiking trail down to your <u>LEFT</u>. Watch carefully for the small park hiking trail stake on your left or you might miss it. It is closer than you think. Walk 290 yards, continue past the South Carolina Monument, and stop at the two tablets for Harker's Brigade on the down slope. Face in the direction of the tablets looking out onto the field.**

 Note: **Refer to the Tour Map inside the front cover as needed.**

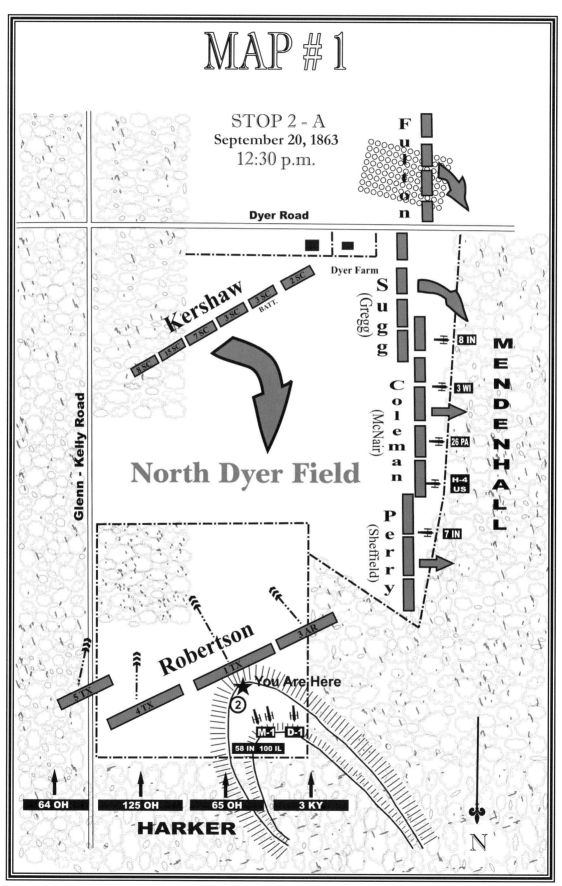

MAP # 1

STOP 2 - A
September 20, 1863
12:30 p.m.

Fulton

Dyer Road

Dyer Farm

Kershaw

2 SC

3 SC
BATT.

3 SC

7 SC

15 SC

8 SC

Sugg
(Gregg)

Coleman
(McNair)

Perry
(Sheffield)

8 IN

3 WI

26 PA

H-4 US

7 IN

MENDENHALL

North Dyer Field

Glenn - Kelly Road

Robertson

3 AR

1 TX

5 TX

4 TX

★ You Are Here

②

M-1   D-1

58 IN   100 IL

64 OH   125 OH   65 OH   3 KY

HARKER

N

STOP 2 - A
Dyer Field and "The Knoll"

The Dyer Field, looking south from Harker's position. Six Confederate brigades could have been visible from this spot. Hood was wounded at the tree line at the center of the photograph.

Before you is one of the most breathtaking views on the battlefield. This peaceful, pastoral scene belies what happened here during the Battle of Chickamauga. In front of you, to the south, is the Dyer field. The field gets its name from the family that farmed it. If you could be transported back to this exact spot at 12:30 p.m. on September 20, 1863, you would see an amazing sight: six Confederate brigades in motion in the field ahead. After their dramatic breakthrough at the Brotherton House, approximately one-half mile to your left-front, Brigadier General Bushrod Johnson's division of three Tennessee brigades (Fulton, Sugg, and McNair) would have been moving from your left to right (east to west), centered on the Dyer Road about 800 yards away. Closer in would have been Brigadier General Evander Law's (Hood's) Division of two brigades (Sheffield's Alabama and Robertson's Texas brigades). Sheffield would also have been moving from east to west about 300 yards before you, but Robertson's Brigade would have been fronting the knoll on which you are now standing and beginning to move up it. The sixth brigade (Kershaw's South Carolina) of Brigadier General Joseph B. Kershaw's (McLaw's) Division would have just been moving out of the tree line 700 yards to your front, wheeling toward this knoll. Kershaw's second brigade (Humphrey's Mississippi) would have still been hidden by the forest in the distance.

The men in McLaw's and Hood's divisions of the Army of Northern Virginia had the good fortune to have drawn new uniforms and equipment on their trip to Georgia. The new uniform coats were of dark blue (some said dark steel gray) with light blue trousers. These neat, new uniforms and the superior style of the equipment caused confusion in both the Confederate and Union ranks in the Dyer field. Kershaw's well dressed and appointed brigade just didn't *look* like the usual threadbare Southern infantry.

The noise would have been deafening. Along the ridge to your right-front (trees block the view today) were positioned 26 Federal cannon commanded by the able Major John Mendenhall. With very little infantry support, they fired for their lives at the advancing Confederate brigades.

The Dyer Field as seen by the Confederates. Harker's position and the South Carolina Monument at the right. Mendenhall's artillery was arrayed along the tree line at the center of the photograph.

Fourteen of these guns would be captured in the next few minutes. Just to your rear, and firing, stood Captain Frederick Schultz's Battery M, 1st Ohio Light Artillery, of six guns, plus the three-gun remnant of Captain Josiah Church's Battery D, 1st Michigan, who had retreated from Brannan's line during the breakthrough at the Brotherton House and rallied here. "The Federal batteries beyond the old field were making our position a veritable hell on earth," a sergeant in Robertson's Brigade recounted. Still, the Confederates advanced.

There was utter confusion in front of the advancing Southern infantry in the Dyer field: the thunder of cannon, routed Union troops by the hundreds (if not thousands), thick smoke and dust, careening wagons and caissons, panicked horses, and a swirling mass of unorganized men. A cacophony of yells, curses, screams of men and horses, cheers, shouted orders, and musket volleys rent the air. It was a scene of absolute chaos. At this point it appeared that nothing could stop Longstreet's infantry from annihilating the Army of the Cumberland.

A trickle of help was on the way, however. A column of Brigadier General Thomas J. Wood's Division (the brigades of Colonels Charles G. Harker, George P. Buell, and led by Colonel Sidney M. Barnes' Brigade of Van Cleve's Division), whose removal from the line had precipitated this crisis, was moving rapidly north on the Glenn-Kelly Road to your left. Barnes was ordered north to support Thomas' line at the Kelly farm. Buell's brigade was caught in the breakthrough and scattered. On taking fire from his right and rear, Harker halted his brigade and he and Wood rode to a point where they could see Confederates advancing into the Dyer field. "When I discovered the enemy in force in the valley south of my command, I at once divined his intention, and appreciated the terrible hazard to our army and the necessity for prompt action," Wood said. "[The enemy] was seeking the rear of

Brigadier General Thomas A. Wood, USA

our solid line of battle, to attack it in reverse, hoping thus to cut our communication with Chattanooga and capture and destroy the bulk of our army."

Wood quickly ordered Harker to form his brigade in the woods perpendicular to the Glenn-Kelly road and advance. A sergeant in the 65th Ohio remarked, "A new line was rapidly formed at right angles to the old, and Harker's brigade was thrown out to check the enemy as one throws a piece of meat to a savage dog to gain time."

Brigadier General Jerome B. Robertson, CSA commanding the Texas Brigade

As Robertson's Confederates marched across the Dyer field and ascended the knoll, they were shaken by blasts of canister from Union artillery. At just that instant, Harker's Federals moved out of the tree line behind you, rushed up to a fence that bordered the north end of the Dyer field, and delivered a devastating volley into the face of the veteran Texas Brigade. A Texan recalled, "That was the meanest, most unsatisfactory place I struck during the whole war. With men staggering and stumbling to the rear covered in blood, some swearing and some calling on God to protect them in their blind endeavor to find shelter from the storm of iron hail, it made me feel like the world was coming to an end then and there."

In just moments, Robertson's brigade was routed and fell back to the trees 700 yards in front of you. At those trees, Major General John Bell Hood, his useless left arm still in a sling from the wound he received at Gettysburg only three months before, attempted to rally his Texans, but fell from his horse, wounded in the right leg by a minie ball. His leg was amputated later that day. His loss at this critical time, as in front of the Round Tops at Gettysburg on July 2, would have a decisive effect on the Confederates' inability to take Horseshoe Ridge.

Major General John B. Hood, CSA. Hood was in tactical command of Johnson's, Law's, and Kershaw's divisions.

A contemporary drawing of Hood's wounding.

As Robertson's Texans retreated, they were also joined by the brigades of McNair and Sheffield, who were enfiladed and could not hold their exposed positions. The strong Confederate attack was on the brink of failing.

The Confederates had no single person coordinating the attacks on Snodgrass Hill after Hood was wounded.

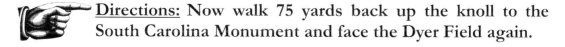 **Directions:** Now walk 75 yards back up the knoll to the South Carolina Monument and face the Dyer Field again.

MAP #2

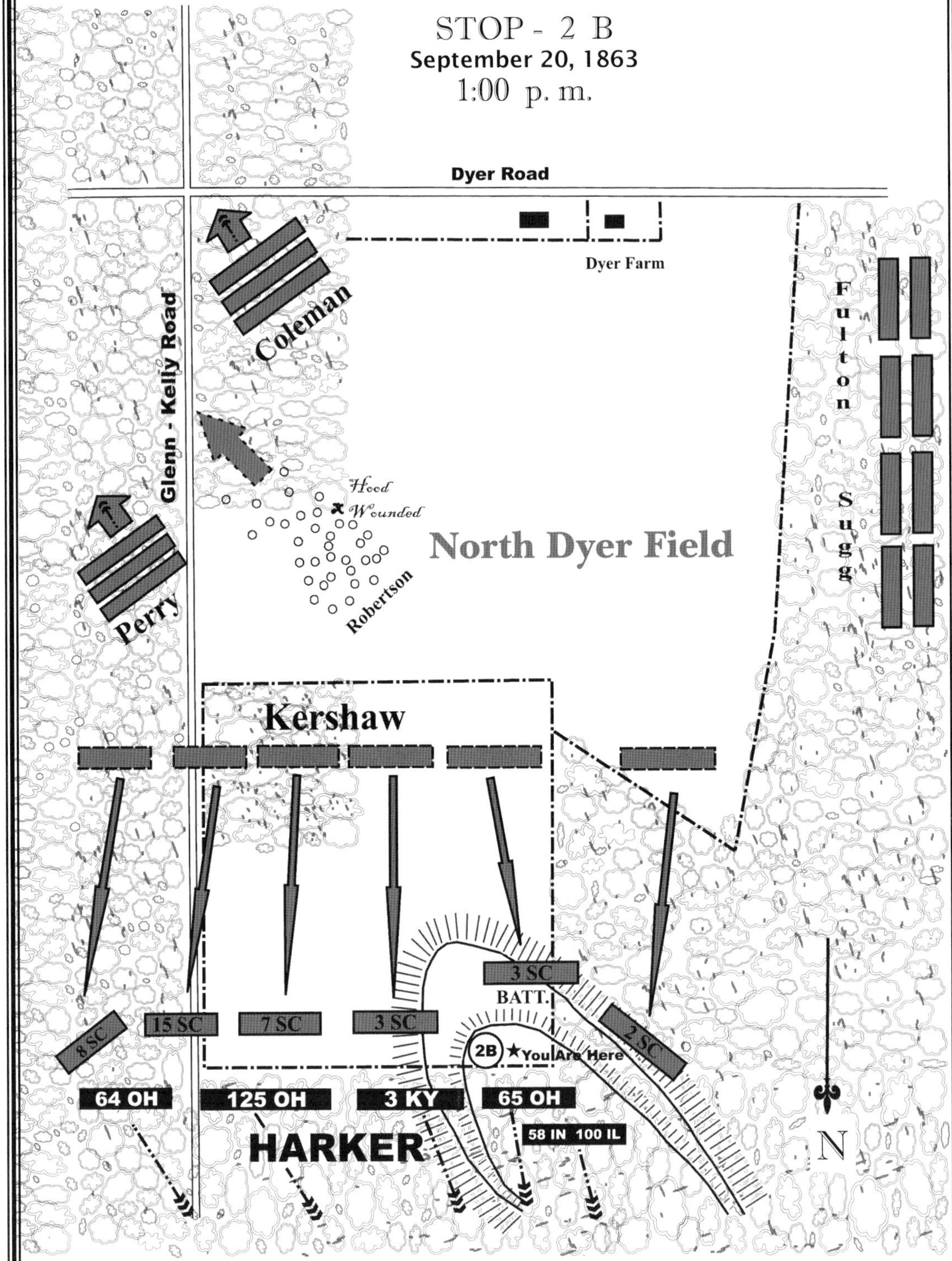

STOP - 2 B
September 20, 1863
1:00 p. m.

Dyer Road

Dyer Farm

Coleman

Glenn - Kelly Road

Hood
Wounded

North Dyer Field

Fulton

Sugg

Robertson

Perry

Kershaw

3 SC

BATT.

8 SC   15 SC   7 SC   3 SC   2 SC

(2B) ★ You Are Here

64 OH   125 OH   3 KY   65 OH

58 IN   100 IL

HARKER

N

STOP 2 - B

Kershaw Attacks

Photograph by Jim Meredith

Schultz's Battery M Monument with the South Carolina Monument in the background.

Joe Kershaw clearly saw the crisis to the north, and the South Carolinian was at the right place at just the right time. Commanding on foot as his horse had not yet arrived from Virginia, Kershaw ordered his brigade of 1,500 men to wheel toward the knoll to the north. In a brilliant tactical move, he ordered the 2nd South Carolina to move to the left to flank the Federal line and ordered the 8th South Carolina to do the same on the right flank. As they advanced, the Confederates expected to take volleys from the Federal line at any moment, but strangely, the blue infantry held their fire.

The reason the Federal troops did not open fire on the Confederates was that Harker, Wood, and their men were confused as to who was approaching them. While many felt it was a brigade of Rebel infantry, some, including Harker and Wood, thought the men in the dark blue

Colonel Charles G. Harker, USA

31

uniforms *might* be Sheridan's division arriving from the south, and did not want to fire into their own men. The color guards of the six Union regiments along the tree line and on the knoll were ordered to stand and wave their flags. If the approaching troops fired on the colors, then the Federals would know for sure who it was. If they held their fire and it *was* Confederate infantry, that decision could doom Harker's brigade. Anxious to the extreme, Harker held his fire.

There was no doubt among Kershaw's infantry as to just who was waving those flags, however. They took the wild waggling of the Federal colors as a challenge to come and get them. "As we were changing front to meet them they seemed to think we were wavering," wrote Lieutenant Colonel Franklin Gaillard, commanding the 2nd South Carolina, "so they waved their flags defiantly at us." Wearing dark uniforms and in the smoke and confusion, Kershaw was able to close within 100 yards of the Federal line, lower his rifles, and fire the first devastating volley.

South Carolina Monument on top of the Knoll

Harker, outnumbered and flanked on both sides, never had a chance. His men fought bravely for a time, but the 2nd South Carolina, coming up the ravine on his right, had flanked his line on top of the knoll. The regiments there were falling like dominoes. The 8th South Carolina caused the 64th Ohio to withdraw on the left flank. Col. Emerson Opdycke's 125th Ohio fought stubbornly, holding on to allow the other regiments of Harker's brigade to withdraw. "The musketry became severe and my losses heavy," wrote Opdycke after the battle. When the fire was hottest, Lt. Charles Clark of Company H shouted in Opdycke's ear: "They can kill us, but whip us never!" But after a few minutes, Opdycke realized to stay would mean capture, so he ordered the 125th to retire, stopping at intervals to fire volleys to keep the Confederates at bay. Wood was so impressed by the bravery of Opdycke's regiment in the Dyer field that he was heard to boast that they had "fought like tigers." From then on, the 125th Ohio was known as "Opdycke's Tigers."

Union General Thomas Wood, the division commander, had his own narrow escape as Harker's men rapidly fell back. Wood was in the middle of Harker's line, behind the Union's 3rd Kentucky, when the 3rd received a tremendous flanking fire and suddenly retreated, losing about 80 men. Wood's horse was shot out from under him. With tongue firmly in cheek, Captain George W. McClure of the 3rd Kentucky recalled, "The brigade was just then driven back. Gen. Wood ran back afoot and made good speed but I being young and muscular, outran and passed him."

Charles Harker's men retreated, but not far. They rallied quickly on Snodgrass Hill, determined to stand to the last. Their most important contribution to the Union army at Chickamauga, however, was the golden hour of time they bought Thomas and Brannan as they formed a defensive line on the soon to be famous ridge behind the Dyer field.

The South Carolina Monument was dedicated on May 27, 1901. Originally, the monument was topped by a bronze Palmetto tree. On several occasions in later years lightning struck the tree, severely damaging it. Tiring of the expense and effort required in replacing their state symbol, South Carolina supplanted the Palmetto tree with the marble shaft you now see. Chickamauga Park Ranger Lee White remarked that he always thought it ironic that, considering South Carolina's place as a pre-Civil War political "lightning rod", their monument here was so often struck by lightning.

Chickamauga Battlefield Park

Directions: Turn to your **RIGHT** and proceed down the trail leading away from the South Carolina Monument. You will pass Garrity's Alabama Battery. **CROSS** the Vittetoe Road and take the trail leading up the hill. Walk 80 yards to the monument for Kershaw's Brigade. Face the monument.

MAP # 3

STOP - 3
KERSHAW'S 1ST ATTACK
September 20, 1863
1:15 p. m.

Snodgrass Field

HARKER

BEATTY

Snodgrass

Battery I

8 SC

Hill 1

Hill 2

BRANNAN

15 SC

Hill 3

21 OH

3 SC
BATT.

3 SC

7 SC

2 SC

③ ★ You Are Here

Kershaw

17 MS   21 MS

Humphreys

Vittetoe Road

N

North Dyer Field

Bushrod
Johnson

STOP - 3

Kershaw's Brigade

The monument to Kershaw's Brigade on the slope of Horseshoe Ridge.
The 3rd South Carolina Regiment marker is to the right.

To the men of Kershaw's brigade, it seemed that nothing stood between them and the top of the ridge—and victory—but broken and retreating Federals. Only one more good push and the day was won. This first climb up Horseshoe Ridge for the Confederates (are you slightly out of breath?) was not an organized attack but the pursuit of a defeated enemy. Kershaw's regiments became separated as they quickly maneuvered to chase the blue infantry up this hill. Remember that Kershaw was on foot, restricting his mobility and impairing his ability to control an entire brigade in the woods and hilly terrain of Horseshoe Ridge. Large gaps developed between his regiments.

Danger lurked ahead on top of the ridge, unseen because of the thick woods. In the crucial hour that Harker had given them, Generals Brannan and Thomas cobbled together a thin but steady line on the broken crests of the ridge. Regiments and fragments of regiments had been placed in line as they arrived, extending the line to the west as rapidly as possible. Harker had rallied on the Union left, on the spur northeast of the Snodgrass House. Men from the brigades of Beatty, Stanley, and Croxton with numerous fragments of other regiments filled in the middle. By a stroke of luck for the Federals, anchoring the right flank on Hill 3 stood the 539 men of the 21st Ohio Volunteer Infantry with their five-shot Colt revolving rifles. They were detached from Sirwell's brigade and had arrived only minutes before.

At 1:15 p.m., Kershaw's men attacked this hastily improvised Federal line. "As we approached this [line] we were met with a very destructive fire," wrote Lt. Col. Franklin Gailliard, commanding the 2nd South Carolina, (to your left). Just to your right, you will see a smaller monument to the 3rd South Carolina, of which Lieutenant Augustus Dickert was a member. Dickert said of this first attack that they "became for a moment a tangled, disorganized mass" as they charged up the hill. The Union rifle fire was withering, and after standing and returning fire for a few minutes, Kershaw ordered his brigade back down the hill to the Vittetoe Road to reform.

After quickly reorganizing his brigade in the road, Kershaw led two more hard-hitting attacks on Horseshoe Ridge, one at 1:45 p.m., and the other at 2:30 p.m. Both attacks swept up the hill and received devastating volleys from Union defenders. In places, after desperate fighting, the South Carolinians reached the top, but Thomas' men fought stubbornly and with great valor. They would not be moved from the ridge crest. All in all, Kershaw's brigade lost fully one-third of its men on Horseshoe Ridge. The brigade losses were particularly high in officers. Longstreet would have to find a way to out-flank the Union position here, and Bushrod Johnson's division was on the way.

Short excursion: Walk about 50 yards up the trail past the Kershaw Brigade monument and you will come out of the woods on Hill 2, at the 35th Ohio monument. You can now get a good feel for how close the lines of battle were on this part of the line. We will return to Hill 2 later in the tour.

Simply put, Kershaw's Brigade was one of the elite formations within the Confederate army. An eminent historian, Ed Bearss, says of the brigade, "Few if any units in the Army of Northern Virginia were more capable or terrible in battle as Kershaw's Brigade." The brigade was organized in April 1861, and served with distinction until it was surrendered by General Joseph E. Johnston in North Carolina on April 26, 1865, some two weeks after Appomattox. Its leader, Joseph Brevard Kershaw, was among the premier combat leaders of General Robert E. Lee's Army of Northern Virginia. Kershaw stood five feet 10 inches tall, with a commanding presence, clear voice, and piercing blue eyes. Pre-war, he was a lawyer and politician by profession, but he was active with the militia and elected colonel of

**Brigadier General
Joseph B. Kershaw, CSA**

the local regiment. He was a veteran of the war with Mexico, returning home deathly sick with fever.

On April 9, 1861, Kershaw was elected Colonel of the 2nd South Carolina Infantry, and served at the bombardment of Fort Sumpter on April 12. He fought his regiment at 1st Manassas in July 1861 and upon the resignation of the brigade commander, Kershaw was appointed to command the brigade in January 1862. Before Chickamauga, he and his illustrious brigade fought at Williamsburg, Savage Station, Malvern Hill, Harpers Ferry, and Antietam. At Fredericksburg in December 1862, he was ordered to take command at the Stone Wall after the mortal wounding of Gen. T.R.R. Cobb. He fought with great gallantry and bravery at Chancellorsville and Gettysburg. At Gettysburg, Kershaw's Brigade suffered 50 percent casualties fighting on the Peach Orchard Road, Rose Farm, and in the Wheatfield. After Gettysburg, the brigade received reinforcements and was rebuilt and refitted.

Rested and at full strength on September 9, 1863, they boarded railroad cars for their trip to the Army of Tennessee. Longstreet at first did not want to take Kershaw's brigade with him. He thought many of the South Carolinians, most of whom had not seen home in more than two years, would take unauthorized leave as the trains made their way slowly through their home state. But Kershaw and his regimental commanders, incensed, gave their personal assurance that their men would arrive in full strength, and they did. Befitting the spirit and gallantry of this proud brigade, he and his men would not be left behind when there was duty to be performed.

Battles & Leaders

Confederate battle line in the woods of Chickamauga.

The monument here was placed to honor the infantry regiments that made up Kershaw's Brigade: 2nd South Carolina, 3rd South Carolina, 3 rd South Carolina Battalion, 7th South Carolina, 8th South Carolina, and the 15th South Carolina. In addition, each regiment's individual marker can be found on the slopes of Horseshoe Ridge.

<u>Directions:</u> Turn and retrace your steps back down the trail to the Vittetoe Road. Turn **RIGHT** on the Vittetoe Road and walk 570 yards to the tablet marking Bushrod Johnson's Division. The tablet will be on your **RIGHT**, at a trail crossing. Turn, face the tablet, and look up the ridge.

<u>On your way</u> you will observe several tablets to Confederate units that attacked Horseshoe Ridge that long September afternoon. If you take the time to read them, their text tells of the severe losses suffered by the various brigades. Sharp eyes might see the three ravines used by the Confederates as they ascended the ridge. The Confederate troops attacked from your left to right, crossing the Vittetoe Road and maintaining constant pressure on the Federals' defensive line on the ridge. The Vittetoe Road was used all afternoon as a landmark to rally and form troops for the many assaults on Horseshoe Ridge.

The 58th North Carolina Monument of Kelly's Brigade (on the left) and the 35th Ohio Monument near the crest of Hill 2.

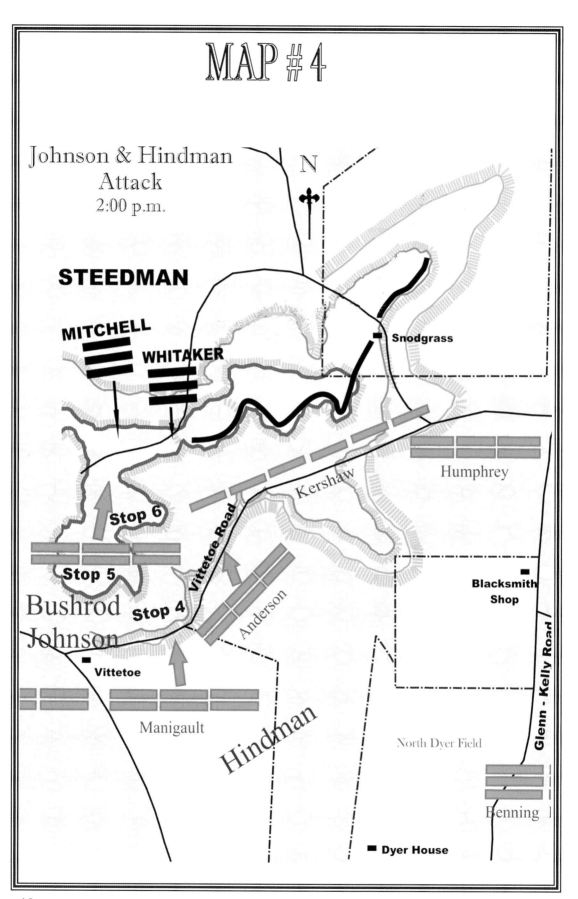

MAP # 4

Johnson & Hindman
Attack
2:00 p.m.

N

STEEDMAN

MITCHELL

WHITAKER

Snodgrass

Kershaw

Humphrey

Stop 6

Stop 5

Vittetoe Road

Bushrod
Johnson

Stop 4

Anderson

Blacksmith
Shop

Vittetoe

Manigault

Hindman

North Dyer Field

Glenn - Kelly Road

Benning

Dyer House

STOP - 4

Bushrod Johnson's Division

Bushrod Johnson's division ascended the ridge at this point, seeking the Union flank. The Vittetoe Road runs right to left in this view.

Exhaustion and casualties now became factors in the Confederate attack on Horseshoe Ridge. While Kershaw's brigade arrived fresh, Johnson's division had been drained by almost constant action every day of the Battle of Chickamauga.

Ohio-born Confederate Brigadier General Bushrod Rust Johnson and his Confederate division had experienced a very busy three days. On September 18, Johnson's division fought Union cavalry under the command of Colonel Robert H.G. Minty for control of Reed's Bridge. On the 19th, he was heavily engaged all afternoon in a confusing battle in the deep woods south and east of the Brotherton farm. In that action, brigade commander Brig. Gen. John Gregg was severely wounded in the neck, and Col. Cyrus A. Sugg took command of the brigade. During the morning of September 20, Johnson's division of three brigades (Fulton, Sugg, and McNair) was in line east of the Brotherton farm. His was the first division in Longstreet's column of three

Ohio born Brigadier General Bushrod R. Johnson, CSA

Confederate divisions waiting for orders to advance. Johnson's Confederates would lead the charge.

Bushrod Johnson's division was ordered forward just after 11:00 a.m. They smashed through the hole in the Federal line left by the departure of Wood's division. Moving due west at the double-quick, the Confederates rushed across the Brotherton farm, through the woods west of the house, and entered the Dyer field. Here, Major General John Bell Hood rode up to Johnson and gave one of the last orders he was to give at Chickamauga: "Go ahead, and keep ahead of everything." The Confederates moved to the ridge west of the Dyer field and attacked Mendenhall's Federal artillery. Johnson's division captured at least 9 of the 26 cannon positioned there. (Five more cannon were captured by other units.) After the fight with Mendenhall, his two remaining Confederate brigades (McNair's brigade had withdrawn all the way back to the Brotherton house) spent more than an hour on the Dyer ridge reorganizing, hauling off captured artillery and packing captured ammunition into depleted cartridge boxes.

Resupplied, and with Major General Thomas C. Hindman's division on the way to reinforce him, Bushrod Johnson moved toward the sound of the battle. When he reached this ground at around 1:30 p.m., his two tired infantry brigades crossed the Vittetoe Road and began to climb the ridge in front of you in search of the Union flank. Brigadier General Patton Anderson's fresh Mississippi brigade of Hindman's division was to Johnson's right. They would find the Federals soon enough.

Optional Short Excursion: Before starting up Horseshoe Ridge, if you will turn 180 degrees and look down the trail, you will see a monument shaped like a cross about 100 yards away. This cross marks the spot where Lt. George W. Landrum of Thomas' staff was killed while trying to deliver a message from Thomas to Rosecrans on the afternoon of September 20. It is a poignant memorial and well worth a visit.

☞ **Directions:** **From the Bushrod Johnson Division tablet, walk up the ridge in the direction the tablets were facing. This is the steepest part of the walking tour. In 140 yards, the trail splits. Take the <u>LEFT</u> trail and walk 15 yards to the two tablets for Gregg's Brigade. Face in the direction of the tablets.**

STOP - 5

Bushrod Johnson Attacks

By the time Bushrod Johnson got his division to this point and in line of battle, they were almost totally exhausted after their three days of constant combat. Here lies the steepest part of Horseshoe Ridge. Johnson needed time to reform his line and allow his men to catch their breath. Artillery was almost impossible to place on Horseshoe Ridge because of the roughness of the terrain, but Johnson could see that guns could be placed on this spur. While his men were getting aligned, he ordered Everett's Georgia and Dent's Alabama batteries to this spot. You can see their positions up the trail to your left.

During this time of reorganization, Brigadier General Patton Anderson's brigade from Hindman's division arrived to the rear of Johnson's position. Johnson ordered Anderson's Mississippians to the right to fill up the space between his command and Kershaw's brigade. The three brigades of Fulton, Sugg, and Anderson would attack the ridge together.

At 2:00 p.m., the three brigades advanced, though the styles of attack were completely different. Anderson's troops were fresh and eager for the fight. They rushed impetuously up the ravine to Hill 3. Johnson's troops, exhausted at having been in almost continuous combat for three days and

Everett's Georgia (left) and Dent's Alabama (background) batteries supported Johnson's division in their attacks on Horseshoe Ridge.

having suffered numerous casualties in both men and officers, moved more slowly and cautiously.

Unfortunately, Anderson ran into the rapid-fire Colts of the 21st Ohio. The Mississippians gave as good as they got. The sound of battle swelled to a roar. Johnson, moving slowly to the next ridge, received only desultory fire from stragglers. Little did he know as he moved forward to the next ridge that a hurricane of blue infantry was sweeping up the opposite side of the ridge from the north. Granger had arrived just in time.

Directions: Turn to your LEFT and continue up the trail. You will pass the positions of Everett's and Dent's batteries. What looks like a tombstone on your right along the way is not a grave. There is no soldier buried here. It is a memorial to Jonathan W. Bull of the 3rd Tennessee who was killed here September 20. Just past Dent's battery, the trail makes a 90 degree turn to the right. Walk 125 yards farther down the trail and stop in front of the monument for Manigault's Brigade.

Jonathan W. Bull Memorial
3rd Tennessee Regiment,
killed on the afternoon of
September 20, 1863.

STOP - 6

Manigault's Brigade
"The air seemed alive with bullets."

After Johnson's first attack failed, Manigault's Brigade assaulted Horseshoe Ridge at 3:00 p. m. in concert with Deas' Brigade.

Brigadier General Arthur M. Manigault's brigade consisted of the 24th, 28th, and 34th Alabama, plus the 10th and 19th South Carolina. Like Patton Anderson's brigade, it was also a part of Gen. Thomas Hindman's division. His brigade, along with Hindman's third brigade under the command of Brigadier General Zachariah C. Deas (pronounced "days"), did not arrive and get into action until 3:00 p.m. Manigault's left flank was about here at the monument, with the rest of his brigade to the right of this point. Deas' brigade was to the left of this point. By the time they attacked, the Federals of Steedman's division of Granger's Reserve Corps was solidly in line on the ridge to your front.

Deas and Manigault overlapped the Union flank, but the rough terrain and the tenacious Federal defense kept the Southerners from exploiting their advantage. Battery M, 1st Illinois Union artillery held the opposite ridge, and blasts of double canister knocked big holes in the Confederate brigades. McNair's brigade rejoined Bushrod Johnson's division after being driven back in their 2:00 p.m. assault and Johson joined this Confederate attack. They attacked on Manigault's right, but nothing could withstand the withering volleys of Steedman's two fresh brigades. Manigault wrote:

"Our men at the word of command, at 3 o'clock, went boldly forward, descending a hill into the gorge and advancing up the opposite, Dent's Battery, 6 Napoleon guns, opening behind and above us on the enemy. A steady and rapid fire assailed us as we advanced, both artillery and infantry. After an unavailing effort we were driven back, the enemy in turn charged us, and the battery for a moment was in great danger. But the gunners served their pieces like veterans, and their gallant captain set an example worthy of emulation. Our men who had been charged when in a state of some confusion, and it was

Brigadier General
Arthur M. Manigault,
CSA

an equal chance whether they would stand or run, rallied and drove their assailants back with heavy loss. Taking advantage of the disorder in their ranks, the brigade charged in turn, and gained some distance. Again moving forward, they were driven back a space, and the enemy repeating their first maneuver, but with less success, laid themselves open to another attack. The first ridge was carried, but on a second just as strong, the enemy again rallied and showed fight. From this one they were driven to a third, the fight resembling and being of the same character as that at the first hill. There was no more obstinately contested ground anywhere on that day than at this point. The blood of the men seemed to be up, and there was but little flinching. On several occasions the colors of two of the regiments fell into the enemy's hands, their bearers killed or wounded, but were quickly recovered. For two hours this contest lasted. Our ammunition was expended again and again in many instances, but the men supplied themselves from their dead and wounded comrades, or those of the Yankees, and when it did not suit their own weapons, threw them away and seized their arms. Towards the latter part of the fight, there was scarcely any order preserved, and no defined line. Regiments and companies were inextricably mixed up, and it resembled more a skirmish on a grand scale than a conflict of a line of battle. Officers and men never before or after behaved better, or showed more indomitable pluck. The air seemed alive with bullets, and an officer afterwards remarked to me, 'General, all you had to do was to hold out your hand, and catch them.'"

The fighting was severe all along the line. Because of the broken terrain, the Confederates, try as they might, could not get the brigades to attack in concert, and the Federals brought each individual assault to a stop. Two or three of the Federal regiments counterattacked and the Southern line began to give way. Finally, Union troops beat back the Confederate attack. As a soldier from the 28th Alabama of Manigault's brigade remembered:

"We were now ordered forward and when we got half way up the hill they opened up on us with great fury with grape and canister and with small arms. But we moved steadily on till we got in about twenty yards of their line where we halted and went regularly to work. Here commenced a scene that beggars description, and God forbid that I should ever have to witness such another. The carnage was awful. Men were shot down all around me. I was indeed in the very midst of death. We fought them thus close I suppose about ten minutes when, as if by command, our whole line gave way and we went down the hill like a gang of sheep."

Although ammunition began to run low, the Union line was secure. The Confederates withdrew down the ridge to reform and regroup for another effort. The fight was not over. More Confederate reinforcements were on the way.

Directions: **Continue 130 yards down the trail to the Union line, and stand in front of the large monument to the 121st Ohio. Face to the RIGHT, looking along the ridge at the line of Union and Confederate monuments.**

MAP # 5

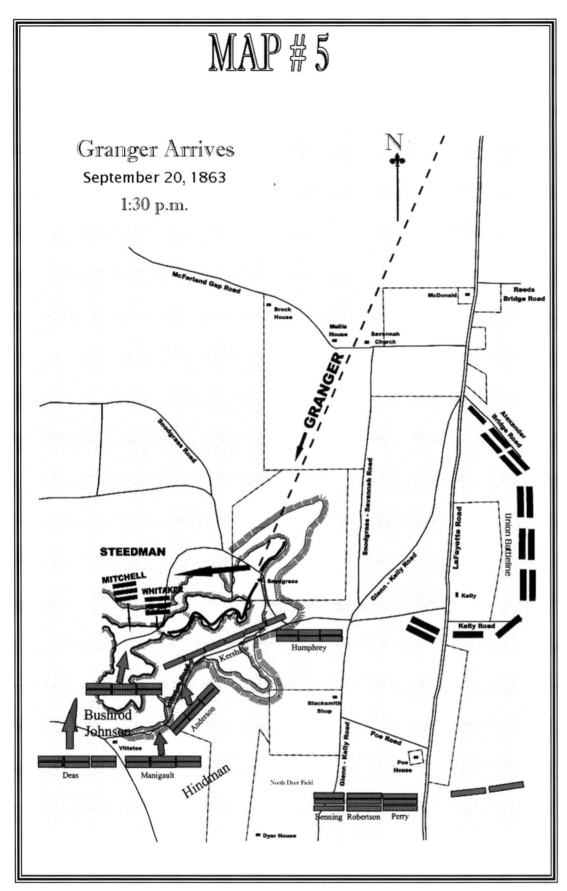

Granger Arrives
September 20, 1863
1:30 p.m.

N

McFarland Gap Road

Brock House

Mullis House

Savannah Church

McDonald

Reeds Bridge Road

GRANGER

Snodgrass Road

Alexander Bridge Road

Snodgrass · Savannah Road

Glenn - Kelly Road

LaFayette Road

Union Battleline

STEEDMAN

MITCHELL

WHITAKER

Snodgrass

Kelly

Kelly Road

Humphrey

Kershaw

Blacksmith Shop

Bushrod Johnson

Anderson

Poe Road

Poe House

Vittetoe

Deas

Manigault

Hindman

North Dyer Field

Glenn - Kelly Road

Benning Robertson Perry

Dyer House

STOP - 7

Granger and Steedman Save the Day

By 1:30 p.m. Union Gen. George Thomas was out of options. Brigadier General Benjamin G. Humphreys' Mississippi brigade threatened his left flank on Snodgrass Hill, and he had received escalating reports of large numbers of Confederates extending far beyond his present right flank on Hill 3 (Bushrod Johnson's division). Harker's brigade could fight the Southerners coming up the hill on the left, but he had no troops that could fight off the large number of Confederates that could wash over his right flank. Thomas' calm demeanor belied the fact that he knew very well the danger he was in. If the Confederates could cross the ridge, get behind his line and cut the gaps leading to Chattanooga, Thomas' XIV Corps in the Kelly field and the units gathered on Snodgrass Hill would be crushed.

Virginia-born Major General George Henry Thomas, USA

Major General Gordon Granger, USA

Thomas had been in the Snodgrass Hill area since about noon and had so far been able to hold the Confederate onslaught at bay. Harker's fight in the Dyer field had given him time to construct a defensive line on the high ground. At 1:30 p.m., he was out of men with which to reinforce his line. The battle had reached a moment of supreme crisis.

From his headquarters behind Snodgrass Hill, Thomas and his staff watched a plume of dust moving closer and closer to their position, marking the approach of troops. But were they Federal or Confederate? Thomas knew that Major General Gordon Granger,

49

with his Reserve Corps, stood to the north guarding Rossville Gap. Possibly the dust could be coming from Granger's corps marching to the battlefield. However, Thomas knew that surprises could and did occur on the battlefield. The approaching soldiers might be Confederates. Thomas had seen Kershaw and the dark uniforms in the Dyer field. Plus, he knew Nathan Bedford Forrest's cavalry was lurking somewhere on his left flank. If the dust signaled Confederates, the day was lost.

With the thunder of battle on the hill above him, Thomas, his legendary calm now showing a little strain, raised his field glass to his eye when the mysterious column came into view to the north across the Mullis and McDonald fields. Whether it was nerves or a balky horse, Thomas could not steady the glass sufficiently in order to identify the approaching troops. "Take my glass, some one of you whose horse is steady, and tell me what you see," Thomas said. One of the aides took the glass and looked. The aide could identify infantry, and he *thought* it was Federal infantry, but dust covered the uniforms and at this distance he couldn't be sure. The tension grew almost unbearable. Thomas then turned to Captain Gilbert M. Johnson of the 2nd Indiana Cavalry. "Captain Johnson, ride over there and report to me who and what that force is," Thomas ordered. (This moment is perfectly captured in Dale Gallon's painting, *The Rock of Chickamauga*, which is used for the cover of this book.)

Johnson rode quickly across the fields to the approaching column. Confederate skirmishers fired at him along the way. Thomas watched as Johnson returned with the best news possible: It's Granger!

Granger's Reserve Corps normally consisted of three divisions, but at the Battle of Chickamauga he had only three brigades available, with the rest of his Corps assigned other duties to the rear of the army. At 11:00 a.m., hearing the sound of battle moving dangerously westward, he and his division commander, Brigadier General James B. Steedman (pronounced *"Steadman"*), decided to move. Granger left Col. Daniel McCook's brigade to guard the Rossville Gap leading to Chattanooga and marched without explicit orders to Thomas' assistance with Steedman's division of two brigades, some 4,000 men. They brought with them 95,000 rounds of ammunition, a godsend to the Federals who were running low on ammunition fighting for their lives on Horseshoe Ridge.

Granger's going to Thomas' assistance without orders is one of the legendary stories of the Battle of Chickamauga. Had he not done so, the ending to the Union stand on Horseshoe Ridge would have been written differently. Granger and Steedman deserve much credit for using initiative and good judgment in "marching to the sound of the guns."

History has ranked Granger's arrival as the most dramatic of the day, but equally important, and often overlooked, was the arrival of Col. Ferdinand Van Derveer's brigade of Brannan's division. This fine brigade reported for duty around 2:30 p.m. (We will cover this brigade's activities at Stop 10.) Thomas now had reinforcements. Would it be enough?

Thomas moved quickly. First thinking to order Steedman's division to plug the half-mile gap between his Snodgrass Hill and Kelly Field lines, instead he ordered Granger to rush Steedman's two brigades to the Union right flank. "My men are fresh, and they are just the fellows for that work," said Granger, who knew of the danger ahead. "They are raw troops, and they don't know any better than to charge up there." Steedman gave the order to move out to his two brigades led by Brigadier General Walter C. Whitaker and followed by Colonel John G. Mitchell. They went up Horseshoe Ridge at the double-quick.

The ground you are standing on was witness to some of the most crucial and dramatic moments of the Civil War. In a matter of 30 minutes, the Army of the Cumberland was saved from disaster. Although neither knew it at the time, Bushrod Johnson's Confederates and James Steedman's Federals were in a race for the possession of this spot. If Steedman won the race, the Federals might hold Horseshoe Ridge until Thomas could extradite what was left of the Army of the Cumberland and join Rosecrans in Chattanooga. If Johnson's Confederates won, Thomas would be flanked from his Horseshoe Ridge line, and his Kelly house line would be taken from the rear.

Steedman won by seconds.

MAP # 6

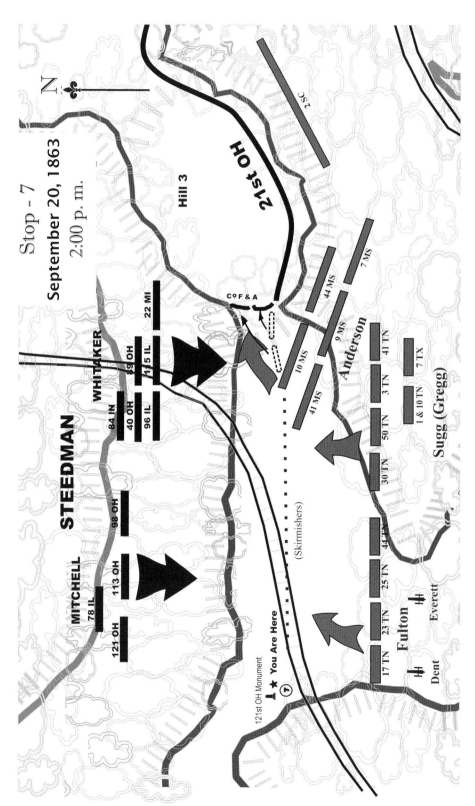

Stop - 7
September 20, 1863
2:00 p. m.

Steedman's line looking east. Mitchell's Brigade ascended the ridge from the left, while the Confederates attacked from the right. Note the Tennessee Monument just visible on the right.

As you look along the ridge at the line of monuments, notice that the ground falls away steeply on both sides. Steedman formed Whitaker's brigade at the bottom of the ridge on your left about 500 yards away. Mitchell's brigade passed Whitaker's and began to form on Whitaker's right. Because of the proximity of Johnson's Confederates, Steedman ordered Whitaker to charge up the ridge before Mitchell's brigade was ready. Mitchell, although forming his lines on the run, lagged several minutes behind Whitaker's advance.

Look to your right. Bushrod Johnson's Confederates advanced cautiously from the low ground below this ridge with the intent of flanking the Union line. Farther in front of you, about 500 yards away, Anderson's Confederates were engaged in a savage attack on the 21st Ohio on Hill 3. Whitaker's Federal brigade, on the charge, crashed into Anderson's Mississippians. Both sides exchanged deadly volleys at close range. Whitaker suffered an abdominal wound from a spent bullet, and every member of his staff was hit within the first minutes of contact. The 22nd Michigan of Whitaker's brigade charged over Hill 3, through the 21st Ohio, and into Anderson's Confederates. The shock of unexpected Federals on their left flank caused the Mississippians to fall back. In spite of shouted orders from Lt. Col. William Sanborn to halt, the 22nd Michigan followed the Confederates all the way to the foot of the ridge, where blasts of canister from Everett's and Dent's batteries up on the ridge stopped them. Sanborn was shot from the saddle, and the color bearer of the 22nd fell dead, his chest ripped open by artillery. Another member of the color guard grabbed the flag from the dead color bearer but was immediately shot through the head. Still another took the flag and had his arm taken off by a solid shot. The 22nd Michigan suffered more than 100 casualties in the first two minutes of this, their first battle. Another of Whitaker's regiments, the 96th Illinois, also lost 100 men in only twenty minutes.

Kershaw now counterattacked the Federals in order to cover the withdrawal of Anderson's brigade, resulting in the 2nd South Carolina pushing the 22nd Michigan back to the top of Hill 3. The 2nd South Carolina then reached the crest of Hill 3, but after desperate fighting had to fall back. The fighting seesawed for control of the ridge. Only fifteen minutes had elapsed from the first volley, a lifetime to those involved.

By Alfred R. Waud

"Steedman's Charge at Snodgrass Hill"

Confederates from Fulton's brigade of Bushrod Johnson's division reached the ridge in front of you and threatened to turn Whitaker's right flank. Just at that moment, Mitchell's Union brigade swept up the ridge on your near-left taking Fulton's exhausted Confederates in flank and drove them from the ridge. Again, Everett's and Dent's Confederate batteries kept the Union brigades at bay by firing canister at the ridge. At 2:45 p.m., the Confederate attack ended. The gray infantry of Sugg and Fulton withdrew to the opposite ridge.

In the thirty minutes since they had left the Snodgrass field at a run, the 4,000 men of Steedman's division suffered 600 casualties, pushed the Confederates off the ridge, and saved the Union right flank. Both sides fought desperately. Good fortune, timely arrival, and hard fighting had saved the Federal Army.

Steedman led from the front in the fight. Early in the attack he had his horse shot out from under him. Taking a bad fall, he bound up his bleeding head and hands, drew his sword, and commanded on foot. Steedman was everywhere, exposing himself where the danger was greatest. At the battle's height, an officer, knowing the next few minutes might be the general's last, asked Steedman if he had any last words. Hatless and bleeding from his head and hands, Steedman (reminder: *"Steadman"*) thought a second, looked at the officer and replied, "By Gawd, see to it that those damned reporters spell my name with two ees!" then turned back to the battle.

**Brigadier General
James B. Steedman, USA**

When the report that Steedman had held the line came back to Thomas' headquarters in the Snodgrass field, Thomas enthusiastically grasped Granger's hand and said, "Fifteen minutes more, General, might have been too late." Later, when Thomas saw the blood-covered Steedman, he said with great emotion, "Steedman, you have saved the army." Thomas had held by the slimmest margin, and he knew it.

The Confederates reformed quickly, and Johnson, reinforced by Manigault's and Deas' brigades, attacked again at 3:00 p.m. (Stop 6). For the next two hours, the Federal line withstood strong attacks by the Southern brigades. For the most part, the Federal infantry fought prone behind any type of small breastwork they could fashion. They took surprisingly few casualties while inflicting severe losses on the attacking Confederates. It was charge and countercharge. The noise was deafening. "The firing of the musketry was so incessant that the ear could not distinguish the separate discharges," wrote a Federal soldier. At times the Southerners would briefly pierce the

Union line, only to be driven back. One Southerner recounted, "We fought them nearly hand-to-hand, using [the] dead for breastworks and their cartridges and guns when ours would become [too] heated."

For thirty minutes the two sides fought for control of the ridge, then Deas and Manigault's Confederates were forced to withdraw. Around 4:00 p.m., Johnson's and Anderson's brigades farther along the line also had to quit the ridge. The attacks had been driven home by the Confederates with great bravery and gallantry, but the stubborn Union line forced back every one with sheets of rifle and artillery fire.

Back at the Snodgrass field, many of the staff officers around headquarters were unsure if Brannan and Steedman's line could hold against the furious Confederate assaults. Every charge seemed stronger than the last. One staff officer, about to leave to carry a message from Headquarters to another part of the line, asked Thomas, "General, after delivering your order, where should I report to you?" Thomas was insistent, "Here, sir, *here*."

Stop 7
121st Ohio Monument

The monument next to where you are standing belongs to the 121st Ohio Volunteer Infantry of Mitchell's brigade, Steedman's division. This regiment was mustered into service on September 11, 1862, and was commanded at Chickamauga by Lieutenant Colonel Henry B. Banning.

Before Chickamauga, the regiment had seen action at the Battle of Perryville, making it one of the few veteran regiments of Steedman's division.

No pictures of battles were taken during the Civil War. In order to preserve their memories, veterans designed bronze bas reliefs to place on the monuments to depict their action on the battlefield. The one here on the 121st monument is one of several to be found on the battlefield, and one of the best. Look for the bas reliefs as you walk the battlefield. They are surprisingly realistic, wordlessly telling their dramatic stories.

Also notice the singular shape of the monument, it is angled away from the line in a shallow "V". This signifies that the 121st Ohio was the end of the Union defenses on Horseshoe Ridge on September 20, 1863, and that they had "refused" their line, preventing the Confederates from gaining the ridge.

After the Civil War, the old soldiers would argue about who did what during the battles: "Who fired the first shot?" or, "What regiment fought the hardest?" The 121st Ohio was involved in a controversy with the 96th Illinois over whose regiment held the Union far right on Horseshoe Ridge. Both regiments vehemently defended their claim to the honor. The truth of the matter was that the 96th Illinois had been split. In all the fighting and confusion, three companies of the regiment had fought to the right of the 84th Indiana, farther down the line. They would fight there for the remainder of the battle, unknown to the rest of the regiment. The highest ranking officer remaining, Captain Borden Hicks, rallied approximately 100 men around the regimental flag. At the time, he thought they were all that was left of the 96th. Eventually he was ordered to the right of the 121st Ohio, to bolster that part of the line. Battery M, 1st Illinois Light Artillery, was also to the right of the 121st Ohio. The 121st could claim that they were the last *full* regiment in line, but if you walk a few yards down the trail behind the 121st monument and past the two guns of Battery M, you will see the monument for the 96th Illinois; placed there *after* the Ohioans had placed their monument!

The Tennessee Monument

Directions: Walk down the ridge past the monuments to Mitchell's brigade. Notice the scattering of Confederate monuments interspersed with the Union monuments. Of special note, on your right you will see the Tennessee State Monument, dedicated on May 19, 1898. Take care to **NOT** walk down the road, but bear to the right to walk between the monuments and the woods. You will begin to discern a trail that will lead up to Hill 3. The Confederate artillery on this ridge was placed here after Steedman retreated. Two guns each of Dent's and Everett's batteries were moved forward and harassed the Union withdrawal. Follow the trail up the hill to the pyramid of cannonballs that marks Granger's Headquarters. (Most likely Granger was never here. He kept his headquarters in the Snodgrass field with Thomas.) You are standing on Hill 3. Stand at "Granger's Headquarters" and face **RIGHT** in the direction the Federal troops were facing.

Tennessee veterans at the dedication of the Tennessee Monument, May 1898

STOP 8 - A

Hill 3

The western side of Hill 3

Here on this rocky hill, and on the ridge to your left, the 21st Ohio Volunteer Infantry Regiment made one of the epic stands of the Civil War. If the battle of Gettysburg has the 20th Maine on Little Round Top, then the Battle of Chickamauga has the 21st Ohio on Horseshoe Ridge.

When Longstreet's gray infantry broke through the Union line at the Brotherton farm at 11:15 a.m., the 21st Ohio Volunteer Infantry Regiment was already on Snodgrass Hill. The regiment was a part of Colonel William Sirwell's brigade of Negley's Federal division. Negley had been ordered to organize a reserve of infantry and artillery for the army. He positioned Sirwell's brigade along the road facing north next to the Snodgrass cabin. As Brannan's battered Federal division reformed on Snodgrass Hill after Longstreet drove them from their original position north of the Brotherton house, Brannan requested the loan of the 21st Ohio from Sirwell's brigade. Negley agreed to the loan, whereupon Brannan ordered the 21st Ohio to the right flank of his improvised line on Horseshoe Ridge. The regiment fought on Brannan's right all during that fateful Sunday afternoon.

Strangely, sometime after 12:30 p.m., Negley gathered up the remainder of his division, plus stragglers from other regiments and around 35 to 40 pieces of artillery, and marched off the battlefield. The artillery, 2,500 infantry, plus the ammunition wagons that went with Negley would be sorely missed in the battle for Horseshoe Ridge. Why he left is a mystery and controversy to this day. Negley never commanded combat troops again.

The 21st Ohio was the right regiment in the right place at the right time. Commanded by Lieutenant Colonel Dwella Stoughton and superbly trained, seven companies out of ten of the 21st Ohio were armed with the five-shot, cylinder-fed, .56 caliber Colt revolving rifle. This gave them tremendous firepower advantage over

The Colt 1855 five-shot revolving rifle. Their tremendous firepower advantage was decisive in allowing the 21st Ohio Infantry Regiment to hold Hill 3.

regularly equipped infantry regiments with their single-shot muzzle-loaders. The 539 men of the regiment were going into the fight well supplied with up to 95 rounds per man, more than twice the amount of ammunition usually carried into battle. Still, all this extra ammunition would not be enough for the fierce fight ahead.

Following somewhat vague orders to connect with Brannan's right flank, Stoughton led his regiment from the Snodgrass house up Horseshoe Ridge to Hill 3. As his regiment formed its battle line just after 1:00 p.m., it began to receive a smattering of fire from Kershaw's skirmishers, who were at that time crossing the Vittetoe Road. Stoughton's line ran from here on Hill 3 to your left across the saddle of the ridge to Hill 2. As soon as its battle line was formed, the 21st began construction of a crude breastwork, using logs, fence rails, limbs, rocks, or any material that came to hand that might protect them.

(If you will look left down the trail, you will spot the monument to the 21st Ohio about 75 yards away. The monument marks the approximate center of the 21st Ohio's line of battle. The monuments you see here on Hill 3 belong to Whitaker's brigade of Steedman's division that arrived later in the fight.)

Only moments after Stoughton's Federals arrived, Kershaw's brigade moved rapidly up the ridge from the Vittetoe Road. The 2nd South Carolina rushed up the ravine between Hill 2 and Hill 3 expecting to meet only light resistance. Instead, the attacking Confederates were met by a solid wall of fire. Caught completely by surprise at the enormous amount of firepower generated by the Colt repeaters, the 2nd South Carolina melted away and retreated quickly back to the Vittetoe Road to regroup. Thinking mistakenly that the Confederates had broken, Stoughton ordered his 21st Ohio to counterattack. The Ohioans stood and charged down the hill. The Carolinians were waiting for them in the Vittetoe Road, however, and the tables turned on the Union infantry. Allowing the Federals to get within twenty yards of the road, the 2nd South Carolina "rose up as one man and poured into them such a volley from our faithful Enfields as to make many of them bite the dust for the last time," recounted one Southern soldier. Now it was the Federal's turn to retreat up the ridge with the 2nd South Carolina in hot pursuit. The Confederates reached the Union breastworks at the crest, but could not stand long under the destructive fire of the Colt repeaters and had to withdraw again. Kershaw regrouped his brigade in the Vittetoe Road for a more organized assault on Horseshoe Ridge. The 21st Ohio settled behind their breastworks for a determined defense of the ridge crest.

2nd South Carolina Monument on Hill 3

Directions: Walk approximately 20 yards forward and slightly to your left and stand by the small stone marker dedicated to the 2nd South Carolina Infantry.

Approximately 70 yards in front of you, on a "small exposed knoll," a Confederate soldier of note from the 2nd South Carolina was killed in this first attack on the 21st Ohio. Sergeant Richard R. Kirkland, the "Angel of Marye's Heights," advanced with his regiment toward this spot. Nine months earlier at the Battle of Fredericksburg, Kirkland, at great risk to himself, had crossed the stone wall at the foot of Marye's Heights and carried canteens of water to the Federals who had been shot down. For ninety minutes, the Federal soldiers held their fire while Kirkland ministered to their wounded. Dedicated in 1965, and commemorating this selfless act of mercy, there is a beautiful statue to Kirkland in front of the Stone Wall at the Fredericksburg National Military Battlefield Park. Kirkland fought at Fredericksburg, Chancellorsville, and Gettysburg, where Kershaw's brigade lost half of its men.

On this September Sunday, he had moved with his South Carolina regiment across the Dyer farm and up the ridge beyond it. Kirkland and his two friends, Arie Niles and James Arrants, were slightly ahead of the 2nd South Carolina when they reached an exposed knoll on the slope of Hill 3. The devastating volley from the 21st Ohio stopped the regiment's advance. A second volley quickly followed the first, and the regiment began to retire. Despite the warning of his comrades, Kirkland turned to fire on the advancing Federals and was shot in the chest. Niles and Arrants ran immediately to Kirkland to bear him from the field, but with blood running from his chest and mouth, he gasped, "No, I am done for. You can do me no good. Save yourselves and tell my father I died right." The "Angel of Marye's Heights," and survivor of so many battles of the Army of Northern Virginia, died here on Horseshoe Ridge.

Sergeant Richard R. Kirkland,
2nd South Carolina,
"The Angel of Marye's Heights,"
killed in the first attack of
Kershaw's Brigade on Hill 3.

Sgt. Kirkland is buried in Quaker Cemetery in Camden, South Carolina, only a few steps from his commander—General Joseph B. Kershaw.

Author's note: There is disagreement regarding where Kirkland was killed and his rank at the time of the Battle of Chickamauga. Many books on the battle have Kirkland killed on the Dyer field knoll. However, this author feels, along with others, that Kirkland was killed here on Hill 3, since eye-witness accounts mention "the advancing enemy." Harker's men did not advance against Kershaw, though the 21st Ohio did counterattack. In Sgt. Kirkland's service record he is listed as first sergeant, not lieutenant. I have found no official report listing him as acting 3rd lieutenant.

There is also a new controversy about whether Kirkland even went over the stone wall at the Battle of Fredericksburg to minister to the Federal wounded. It makes interesting reading. I will leave it up to you to research this controversial subject and form your own opinion.

Before leaving the 2nd South Carolina monument, note the two monuments behind you. They are for the 22nd Michigan and the 89th Ohio which were attached to Whitaker's brigade, Steedman's division. Along with the 21st Ohio, they were captured here on Hill 3 by the Confederates in the closing minutes of the battle. (We will discuss this at Stop 9.)

Directions: **Turn and walk 70 yards down the trail to the 21st Ohio monument. Face the monument and look down the ravine in the direction the Federal infantry faced.**

Michigan at Chickamauga

Hill 3 ca. 1895

The 21st Ohio held this line against repeated attacks
by the Confederates on the afternoon of September 20, 1863.

The 21st Ohio Monument is in the center of the photograph.
The Confederates attacked uphill from the right.

Major Arnold McMahan.
After Lieutenant Colonel Dwella Stoughton was mortally wounded, McMahan assumed command
of the 21st Ohio. At 7:00 p.m., McMahan was captured along with most of the 21st Ohio
and its colors. He was exchanged on March 1, 1864, and commanded the 21st Ohio
for the remainder of the war. Regrettably, there is no known photograph of Stoughton.

Because of the tremendous firepower advantage held by the 21st Ohio, they were able to defend a much longer line than a regularly armed infantry regiment. The Ohioans' left flank extended around the curve of the trail to your left all the way to the cleared area. To the right, it extended to and just over Hill 3. This was a thin single line, not a double line of infantry with elbows touching. The 21st Ohio fought kneeling or prone behind their small breastwork, defending this line against the Confederates' constant heavy attacks.

Kershaw's initial attack on the ridge at 1:15 p.m. was followed closely by a more organized assault at 1:45 p.m. Again, a wall of fire met the South Carolinians as they charged up the ridge. By practice, the Confederates would customarily absorb the Federals' first volley and then

The 21st Ohio Monument on Horseshoe Ridge. This regiment fought heroically for six hours until, out of ammunition, it was captured on Hill 3 along with the 22nd Michigan and the 89th Ohio.

rush ahead for the final charge before the Federals could reload. But because of the repeating Colts, the Confederates could take no more than a step or two before another devastating volley would explode in their faces, followed closely by yet another. No infantry could stand under this fire. Even though some brave Confederates once again reached the crest of the ridge, after a few minutes Kershaw's gray soldiers had to withdraw from the Ohioan's front in the face of this tremendous firepower. It is doubtful whether any Union regiment armed with the usual Springfield or Enfield single-shot rifles could have held this position.

The South Carolinians had barely retreated down the ridge before another heavy blow hit the 21st Ohio. At 2:00 p.m., Anderson's brigade of

Mississippians hit the right flank of the regiment on Hill 3. The roar of battle once more reached a crescendo. Lt. Col. Stoughton was shot by a Southern sharpshooter. Command of the 21st Ohio was assumed by Major Arnold McMahan. (Stoughton's left arm was shattered. He died of his wound on November 19, 1863.) Anderson's "gallant and impetuous charge" threatened to turn the Ohioans' right flank. To defend this flank, McMahan ordered companies A and F pulled back perpendicular to the Union line on Hill 3. Even armed with the Colts, two companies could not hold long against an entire Confederate brigade. At 2:00 p.m., when the battle looked most desperate, Steedman arrived in the nick of time on the right of the 21st Ohio and saved the regiment's flank. Before the ridge could be cleared of Confederates, Kershaw moved up the ridge at 2:45 p.m., and for the third time the 2nd South Carolina attacked the 21st Ohio here.

For the soldiers of the 21st Ohio, the attacks seemed continuous. Each appeared more desperate and dangerous than the one before. Lieutenant Wilson Vance of the 21st Ohio wrote: "Our assailants seemed to under-stand that our frail line was all they had to overcome to reach the rear and very heart of the horseshoe formation. There was that peculiar fierceness in the manner of the assault that men show when they realize that the supreme opportunity has presented itself, and are determined not to let it slip. And our boys could do nothing but set their teeth and fight, as for their lives."

Casualties mounted. Because of the high rate of fire of the Colts, the men began to run out of ammunition. They took rounds from the cartridge boxes of the dead and wounded. Sgt. John Bolton accompanied a detail to the Snodgrass house to retrieve the cartridge boxes from the wounded 21st Ohio soldiers at the field hospital there. The thin line of the 21st Ohio got thinner, but still they held. One captured Confederate soldier who had been brought into the regiment's dwindling line looked around in shock at the numbers of men and exclaimed, "Where are the rest of your men? My God! We thought you had a division here!"

The 21st Ohio Infantry expended 43,550 rounds of ammunition in its fight for Horseshoe Ridge.

An officer in the 21st Ohio left this account after the battle: "Another man had two or three fingers shot off his right hand, and he instantly flashed into temporary insanity. He cursed and reviled the Johnnies with the most horrible and grotesque profanity that ever came from man's worst imagination, dancing and gyrating almost comically. Then he sought a wounded comrade, who, lying upon the ground and unable to stand upright, could still load his rifle. Thus aided, the crazy man kept on firing and shouting and cursing till the loss of blood made him faint."

The drought of that summer had been the worst in years. It was not long until the black powder discharges from the weapons had set the woods on fire in places in front of the regiment. Volunteers went forward to retrieve the wounded; some were burned piteously.

Bodies, parts of bodies, blood, gore, smoke, fire, thunderous noise, screams of the wounded, incoming artillery fire from Dent's and Everett's Confederate artillery, and constant charges by the gray infantry all combined to create a living hell on earth here on this slope in front of the 21st Ohio. The regiment held on, but the Confederates noticed that its rate of fire had slowed noticeably. Casualties depleted the regiment. In addition, the black powder rifles became fouled by powder residue and rendered hard to load. There was no acid at hand to clean them. Some of the men resorted to urinating down the barrels and over the cylinders in order to clear them of powder residue. In addition, soldiers were running out of ammunition. Under Maj. McMahan's orders, as each soldier fired his last round, he was directed to walk down the ridge to reform in the ravine below Hill 3. Some Federals tried to fire .58 caliber ammunition in their .56 caliber Colts. Some of the rifles exploded. The more adventurous men found that if they attached bayonets to their rifles, the barrels would not shatter. By 4:45 p.m., hardly any members of the 21st Ohio had enough cartridges left to fill the cylinders of their Colts. The heroic stand of the 21st Ohio was almost at an end.

At this point in the battle, Brigadier General William Preston's fresh Confederate division entered the fight for Horseshoe Ridge. Preston's 4,463-man division consisted of three brigades under the command of Brigadier General Archibald Gracie Jr., Colonel Robert C. Trigg, and Colonel John H. Kelly. At 4:45 p.m., Kelly's brigade attacked Hill 3. The 21st Ohio let the Confederates close to within sixty yards and then fired their final volley. Completely out of ammunition, the Ohioans then withdrew to the reverse slope. Also out of ammunition and falling back to that slope were the 22nd Michigan and 89th Ohio. Kelly's brigade marched to the top of Hill 3. For the first time in the fight for Horseshoe Ridge, the Confederates had a tenuous hold on the high ground.

The stand of the 21st Ohio Infantry Regiment on Horseshoe Ridge was indeed one of the epic defensive stands of the Civil War. It is worth considering that had this regiment failed, Thomas' right flank would have been turned, resulting in the collapse of the Snodgrass Hill/Horseshoe Ridge line. Longstreet could then have moved to attack the Kelly field line from the rear, killing or capturing most of the four divisions there. The Union defeat would have become a Union disaster, the largest of the war.

Had this been the case, it is easy to conceive that the remnants of the Army of the Cumberland would have had to withdraw from Chattanooga, its prize, thus significantly prolonging the Civil War. There would have been no Atlanta Campaign; Atlanta would not have fallen in September 1864. Abraham Lincoln's Republican Party nomination for a second term might have failed (it was never a foregone conclusion), and the election of 1864 might have been won by a candidate tired of the war who would have allowed the South to go its own way.

Much is made of the 21st Ohio's more famous cousin, the 20th Maine and its stand on Little Round Top at the Battle of Gettysburg. Both regiments held the extreme flank of their respective army. Both stood on lonely, rocky hills. Could the North have lost the Battle of Gettysburg or the Civil War (as some say) if the 15th Alabama had driven the 20th Maine off Little Round Top? The answer is an emphatic—**no**. The 15th Alabama was exhausted, suffering from a lack of water, and almost out of ammunition. Elements of the V Corps and almost all of the VI Corps of the Army of the Potomac were within easy reach of Little Round Top, while the Confederates had no unengaged infantry or artillery to use as reinforcements on the field. To put it another way: 300 tired men versus 14,500 fresh troops. Not good odds at all—even for Alabamians. The life expectancy of the 15th Alabama would have been about thirty minutes.

This is not to denigrate the history of the 20th Maine in the least. Theirs was a courageous and momentous stand. So was the stand of the 21st Ohio. One regiment lives in fame, however, while one is largely forgotten. I hope that in the future as many visitors to Chickamauga will visit the monument to the 21st Ohio as visit the 20th Maine monument at Gettysburg—and remember the valiant stands of both.

 **Directions:** Continue down the trail approximately 85 yards until you enter a clearing. Just as you enter that clearing, look to your right: you will see a tablet titled "Close Of The Battle". Stand in front of the tablet, facing down the ravine.

The 21st Ohio Monument guards the ravine up which Kershaw's infantry attacked on September 20, 1863.

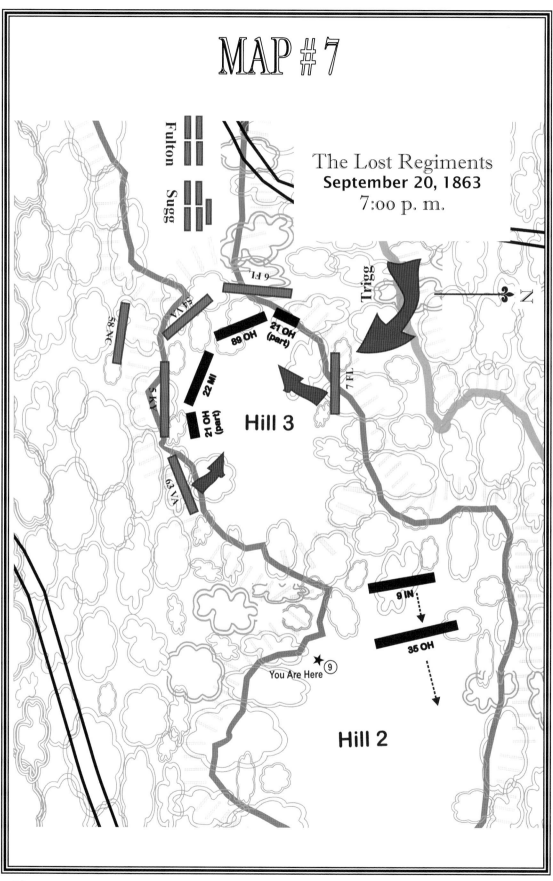

MAP #7

The Lost Regiments
September 20, 1863
7:00 p. m.

Fulton

Sugg

Trigg

N

6 FL

54 VA

58 NC

89 OH

21 OH (part)

7 FL

22 MI

5 KY

21 OH (part)

Hill 3

63 VA

9 IN

35 OH

★ ⑨
You Are Here

Hill 2

STOP 9 - A

The Lost Regiments
and the Close of the Battle

As darkness descended on Horseshoe Ridge, Gen. James Steedman's two Federal brigades to the west of Hill 3 were almost out of ammunition. Having thrown back every attack made against them, some of his units were completely out of ammunition while others had only a round or two left in their cartridge boxes. Lack of visibility had also become a problem. As the sun set, long shadows from the thick woods fell across the battle lines. In addition, thick smoke from gunpowder and brush fires obscured sightlines to only a few yards. Darkness came more quickly in the deep woods than it did in the open fields.

In throwing back charge after charge of Confederate infantry, Steedman's units had become hopelessly intermingled. Regimental lines were in disorder, and even companies were mixed up within the regiments. No one person could exert command over his battle line. In all this confusion, the Confederates showed signs of another attack.

At 5:00 p.m. Confederate division commander Bushrod Johnson, down to about 1,800 men in his three brigades, made another advance. It was not a mad rush in line of battle like the other assaults. Rather, the men advanced steadily in loose order, from tree to tree, firing and keeping steady pressure on the Union brigades of Whitaker and Mitchell. The Union infantry could offer only a sporadic fire in response, and by 5:30 p.m., the Federal line began to give way. At the same time, orders came from Gen. Granger to withdraw. As this order passed down the line, the hard-pressed and out-of-ammunition Federals fell back rapidly, without much thought of coordination. The time was about 6 p.m.—sundown on Horseshoe Ridge.

Bushrod Johnson's infantry now held the crest of the ridge they had been fighting so hard all afternoon to take.

All this is important to understand because the Union units on the ground on which you are standing had not been informed of the withdrawal of Steedman's division. Because of the nature of the Confederate advance and Steedman's sporadic return fire, these units had not heard the loud sound of combat as before. In addition, the fading daylight and battle smoke obscured officers' views of what was happening. Steedman's division had retreated suddenly from the battle line, but no superior officer had thought of informing the Union troops defending Hills 1 and 2. For all they knew, Steedman was still in position holding the line.

Thomas was no longer on the Snodgrass Hill front. At 4:30 p.m., he had received orders from Rosecrans to withdraw to Rossville immediately and take up a defensive position there. Thomas had wanted to hold his Chickamauga lines until dark and then retreat, but the lack of ammunition and growing Confederate pressure led him to the decision to retreat at 5:00 p.m. Leaving Granger in charge of pulling his troops off Horseshoe Ridge, Thomas rode to supervise the withdrawal of what he considered to be the most dangerous part of the retreat: the four Union divisions on the small ridge to the east of the Kelly House.

"The Lost Regiments." Monuments to the 22nd Michigan (foreground), and 89th Ohio on Hill 3. Along with the 21st Ohio, these regiments were captured on Hill 3 at the close of the battle.

Both the 89th Ohio and the 22nd Michigan had been temporarily attached to Whitaker's brigade. These two regiments, under Whitaker's orders, formed a "demi-brigade" under the command of the 22nd Michigan's Col. Herber Le Favour. During the rapid retreat from the ridge, Whitaker informed the four regiments in his brigade but forgot to inform the two attached regiments which remained on Hill 3. They were without orders to withdraw and without ammunition. Whitaker was drunk. Early in the action he had been struck in the abdomen by a ball that did not penetrate the skin. While painful, it was certainly not life-threatening. Nonetheless, Whitaker rode to the rear where he remained for some time recuperating from the shock of being hit and partaking of some liquid courage. When he returned shortly before Steedman's withdrawal, witnesses report his reeling in the saddle and giving bizarre orders. At one point, in answer to a request for more artillery ammunition, he ordered the cannoneers to fix bayonets on their cannon! Sgt. George Dolton of Battery M said, "I do not think, when he left my guns, that he could have told where his command lay."

Le Favour was not about to stay and be captured when the rest of the division had departed so rapidly. He quickly ordered his two regiments to about-face and marched them off Hill 3. He had gone but a few yards when a staff officer ordered him to halt and resume his place on Hill 3, holding it with the bayonet if necessary. The staff officer promised ammunition and reinforcements (neither of which ever came). Le Favour had no choice but to resume his position atop the hill. His men lay down in the gathering darkness and hoped the Confederates would not come.

The heroic 21st Ohio was also ordered by Col. Van Derveer to Hill 3. Virtually without ammunition, they were to hold it at the point of the bayonet. The only reason these three regiment commanders could think of as to why they were sent to Hill 3 with empty cartridge boxes was that they were to be sacrificed in order for the rest of the army to make good its retreat. They determined to hold as long as possible.

Confederate division commander Brigadier General William Preston had committed two of his three brigades to assault Horseshoe Ridge earlier at 4:45 p.m. Kelly's brigade had attacked Hills 2 and 3 (Stop 8), and Gracie's brigade had attacked Hill 1 (Stop 11). Now, he committed his third brigade under the command of Col. Robert C. Trigg on the Confederate far left flank.

When Trigg's Confederates arrived, he and Kelly had a short conference. Kelly told Trigg that if he moved his regiments around to the left and to the back of Hill 3 they could outflank the Federals there, and he would attack from the front. Trigg agreed to the arrangement and his infantry moved out. The hastily improvised plan worked to perfection.

It was almost 7:00 p.m., and the darkness worked to the Confederates' advantage. Five Southern regiments advanced toward and around Le Favour's regiments and the 21st Ohio. Kelly's brigade moved up the ridge from your left, and Trigg's brigade moved up the ridge from your right (the Trigg Brigade tablet is down the small trail to your right). "It was impossible to tell who they were until they got within ten feet of us, when through the gloom we could see that their uniforms were gray," recounted Lt. Edward Scott of the 89th Ohio. "It was too late to do anything even if we had any ammunition." Some members of the 21st Ohio escaped as the 35th Ohio and 9th Indiana fired a volley into the darkness, but Maj. Arnold McMahan and most of his regiment were captured, a bitter end to a most heroic stand. (The 21st Ohio entered the fight commanded by a lieutenant colonel and left the battlefield commanded by a captain: Captain Charles H. Vantine.) The 22nd Michigan shared the same fate. Union Sgt. Marvin Boget wrote: "Just at dusk our ammunition gave out, and the Johnnies had advanced on our right and left as we could tell by the yelling. Finally they closed in on us with guns pointing us in the face and a command to 'throw down your guns and lie down on the ground.' I tell you I wasn't long in obeying." The capture of the regiments was now complete. Some 563 men were reported missing from the three regiments the next day.

Here on Hill 2, all that was taking place in the smoky gloom was a mystery. In answer to a request for reinforcements, the 9th Indiana of Brigadier General William B. Hazen's brigade was detached and led to this spot. (The 9th Indiana's stone marker monument is just behind you.) Hearing loud voices, but not much firing ahead of him in the darkness when he arrived, Col. Isaac Suman, the 9th Indiana's commanding officer, rode out in front of his line to determine just what was happening. It was a mistake. Suman was captured. Suman told the Confederate officer who captured him that he had already been captured once, and when the Rebel dropped his guard Suman was able to escape. Riding quickly back to his regiment, Suman ordered a volley, and the Confederates melted back into the darkness.

Suman, knowing that the Confederates were there in force and unwilling to have his regiment captured, ordered his men to about-face and began to march them back across Hill 2. Lt. Col. Henry V. Boynton, commander of the 35th Ohio, Col. Ferdinand Van Derveer's right flank regiment (Stop 10), mistakenly thought Suman was leaving because of cowardice. Boynton, who had ably assisted in holding this part of the line all afternoon, thought (again mistakenly) the Union line still extended to the right. Suman *knew* that not only were there no Federal troops to the right, but also that Confederate infantry was there in force. A heated exchange ensued in which Boynton loudly called the Hoosiers "cowards" and insulted them and their colonel "in plain language."*** See comments on page 77.**

Suman's veteran troops would not stand to be called cowards by anyone. Calls of "Let's go back, Colonel," and, "Let us go back and fight," rang out. Suman countermanded his orders and marched his regiment back, forming a line across the ridge at this point.

Marker to the 9th Indiana on Hill 2.

The 35th Ohio had refused its right flank across Hill 2, extending its flank past the right of the 9th Indiana. Hearing the crack of twigs in the woods signifying a Southern advance, both the 9th Indiana and the 35th Ohio fired a volley into the darkness, causing the Confederates to withdraw back into the gloomy darkness. This was the last volley fired in the Battle of Chickamauga. To this day there is a debate as to who fired that final volley of the battle. Was it the 9th Indiana or the 35th Ohio?

After this final volley, the 68th and 101st Indiana moved to the right of the 9th Indiana and 35th Ohio. Boynton ordered them to hold until he could withdraw the 9th and 35th. With the whole of the Snodgrass Hill-Horseshoe Ridge line now withdrawn, all four regiments retreated as quickly as possible in the dark, down the hill toward the Snodgrass house.

The Army of Tennessee was victorious. It was their first and only victory of the Civil War. One South Carolina officer of Kershaw's command described the aftermath: "Fires had broken out in the dry woods illuminating the ghastly scene, but also providing light for the hungry Confederates to search abandoned Federal haversacks for food. In the midst of the killed of both sides, they feasted on canned beef, ham, and crackers."

As the exhausted Union survivors stumbled in the moonlight through the woods and over the rough rocky roads north toward Chattanooga, they heard a chilling sound. The two wings of the Confederate Army (Longstreet's and Polk's) had finally come together, and the joyous Graybacks sent up a Rebel yell that would be remembered for decades. General James Longstreet remembered it this way after the war: "The Army of Tennessee knew how to enjoy its first grand victory. The dews of twilight hung heavy about the trees as if to hold down the voice of victory; but the two lines [wings] nearing as they advanced joined their continuous shouts in increasing vol-

Lieutenant General James Longstreet, CSA

ume, not as the burstings from the cannon's mouth, but in a tremendous swell of heroic harmony that seemed almost to lift from their roots the great trees of the forest."

The Battle of Chickamauga had ended.

Before you leave, Stop 9 is one of the best places to see how the curvature of the Horseshoe Ridge crest worked against the Confederate attackers and greatly aided the Federal defenders. As you face the tablet recounting the "Close of the Battle," you are basically looking straight at the 21st Ohio monument that you passed a moment ago, and down the battle line of the 21st Ohio. The Union line extended to the right from here all the way past Hill 3. To your left, the Union battle line extended from here over Hill 2 at almost a *right angle* to the 21st Ohio battle line. It is easy to see that Union infantry here on Hill 2 could fire into the flank of any Confederate unit attempting to assault the 21st Ohio or Hill 3. The irregular shape of the ridge crest is why many Confederates felt that they were receiving fire from the flanks and rear as they attacked.

*A note about Suman from page 75.   Boynton did not know Suman, nor had he ever been in combat with the 9th Indiana. The 9th was a veteran infantry regiment from another corps, fighting with valor at Shiloh, Corinth, Perryville, and Stones River before the Tullahoma Campaign. On the first day of the Battle of Chickamauga, the 9th had advanced into the Brock Field, where it had stood bravely with the rest of Hazen's brigade fighting Maj. Gen. Ben Cheatham's veteran Confederate division. Later on September 19 it had helped repulse the breakthrough of Confederate Maj. Gen. A. P. Stewart's division at the Brotherton farm. Overnight, on the 19th, the 9th Indiana was moved with Hazen's brigade to the Kelly Field line. Early on the morning of September 20, Suman requested of Hazen that he be allowed to build a breastwork to protect his men. Hazen gave his permission, and in addition ordered his whole brigade to do the same. The division commander, Maj. Gen. John M. Palmer, soon ordered the whole division to build breastworks. Whether word spread, orders were given, or the men just heard the ringing of axes, by 9:30 a.m., Thomas' entire line behind the Kelly house was soon protected by log defenses. Suman then led the 9th Indiana all morning of the 20th through the vicious assaults of Patrick Cleburne's division. Should Suman get the credit for thinking of the log breastworks? Who knows? But one fact is clear: Isaac Suman was no coward.

After the Civil War when the various states were deciding where their monuments should go on the Chickamauga Battlefield, the 9th Indiana wanted its monument to be placed here on Horseshoe Ridge. Henry V. Boynton (late commanding officer of the 35th Ohio Infantry) was the battlefield historian and then chairman of the committee that had the final decision as to where each regiment could place its monument. Boynton refused the 9th Indiana permission to place its monument here. Despite appeal after appeal, Boynton steadfastly refused. In 1893 the final verdict was handed down: the 9th Indiana had lost no men on Horseshoe Ridge, and following Boynton's "Brigade and Best Fighting" rule, the monument to the 9th Indiana would be placed in the Brotherton field, and stone markers could be placed in the Brock field, Kelly line, and Horseshoe Ridge. From the heated and harsh words in the smoke, confusion, and darkness on that gloomy Sunday evening in September, Henry V. Boynton could carry a grudge.

Boynton, certainly no coward himself, was severely wounded and awarded The Medal of Honor for his heroic actions during the assault of Missionary Ridge on November 25, 1863.

One final note: After losing so many men in the Brock field, the Brotherton field, and the Kelly farm, the 9th Indiana wanted its monument here on Horseshoe Ridge where it didn't lose a man. The reason is inspiring to us today. Every man in the 9th Indiana went back to the line of battle to face, as they thought at the time, certain death or capture. As a 9th Indiana Infantry historian wrote many years after the war, "Any man can fight a battle he's sure of winning; it takes a hero to fight one he's sure of losing."

<u>Directions:</u> **Turn to your left and walk 40 yards up the small hill. Stop in the middle of the clearing. This is the top of Hill 2. Turn and face the 35th Ohio monument approximately 40 yards to your right.**

STOP 9 - B

You are standing in a cemetery. Somewhere beneath your feet lie the final resting places of George Washington Snodgrass and his wife, Elijah Kelly and his wife, Mrs. Mary McDonald, and many others. This cemetery was in use both before and after the Civil War. When the Chickamauga National Battlefield Park was first established, four observation towers were built in the approximate corners of the battlefield. One tower was located here on this spot. When the towers were dismantled after WWII, the ground was carelessly bulldozed and the graves lost to history.

In view straight ahead stands the monument to Lt. Col. Henry V. Boynton's brave 35th Ohio Infantry. Notice that it seems to stand alone on the most prominent ground on Hill 2. To your left and down the hill are monuments to the other three regiments of Van Derveer's Union brigade, 2nd Minnesota, 87th Indiana, and 9th Ohio. To someone casually viewing the battlefield it would seem Boynton and the 35th Ohio fought here alone. This is the very impression that Boynton wished to leave future generations.

Many monuments on the Chickamauga Battlefield are not placed exactly where the units fought. Civil War brigades fought using the new *Casey's Tactics*, which instructed that in a four-regiment brigade, two regiments would be up front and two regiments would be in reserve in the second line. This would give the brigade commander greater flexibility in the fighting of his brigade. As the park was being formed and locations for monuments being decided upon, no regiment wanted its monument to be placed in the second line. In addition, regiments wanted their monument placed on significant high ground where they could be seen, not in low ground or ravines where the monuments could be overlooked. Close was good enough in some cases.

The monuments to Van Derveer's regiments should be up on this hill. The 35th Ohio fought hard in the low ground farther to the right. The diorama in the Visitors Center depicts the 9th Ohio Infantry's bayonet charge down Horseshoe Ridge, which took place slightly to the left of where the 35th Ohio monument stands. Many of the monuments down the hill to your left should be placed one brigade length to the west. Certainly the battle here was fluid and the regiments fought at different locations along Horseshoe Ridge during that long afternoon. Henry V. Boynton, the most influential person responsible

Chickamauga Battlefield Park.

The Observation Tower on Hill 2, ca. 1935. Note the 35th Ohio Monument to the right.

for the placement of monuments, took the liberty of having the other monuments placed away from that of the 35th Ohio monument. He erected his own regimental memorial on the most prominent ground on Hill 2. Visitors to the old observation tower, and visitors today, see the 35th Ohio monument standing alone.

**Stop 9—B
The 35th Ohio Monument stands alone on Hill 2. Somewhere in this view is the unmarked grave of George Washington Snodgrass and his wife.**

Note: The Kershaw Brigade monument that you visited on Stop 3 is down the trail and only a few yards in front of the 35th Ohio monument.

Directions: Continue downhill in the direction of the beautiful monument that has three soldiers on its top. This is the monument to the 2nd Minnesota of Col. Ferdinand van Derveer's Federal brigade. Go to the front of the monument and face down the ridge.

STOP 10

Hill 2: Van Derveer's Brigade

All along the ridge crest, lying prone behind low breastworks, the Federal infantry withstood attacks of "almost inconceivable fury and persistence," as one Union officer described them. Gen. Joseph Kershaw mounted attack after attack on this part of the Federal line, urging his South Carolina brigade to drive the blue infantry off the ridge. Hand-to-hand combat was relatively rare in the Civil War, despite common perception, but here on this area of Horseshoe Ridge, the Confederate attacks surged time and again all the way to the Federal breastworks, and men grappled with each other for control of the position. The fighting was violent and desperate.

Stop 10
2nd Minnesota Monument

At this point, around 2:30 p.m., the 7th South Carolina of Kershaw's brigade drove its way to the top of the ridge and fought toe-to-toe with the Union defenders. Ensign Alfred D. Clark carried the battle flag of the 7th South Carolina up the ridge and stood in front of the works waving his flag. He was so close that a Federal field officer shouted that any man who could capture that flag would win a captain's commission. Several men sprang forward. Just at that instant, Clark received a mortal wound to the chest. As he fell, seeing Federal soldiers rush toward him, with his last gasp, he threw the flag of the 7th South Carolina behind him to his friends, thus saving it.

7th South Carolina Marker on Horseshoe Ridge. Ensign Alfred D. Clark was the color-bearer for this regiment.

After the War, then General J. S. Fullerton, who was Major Fullerton at Chickamauga and served as chief of staff to Gen. Gordon Granger, was a member of the Chickamauga Battlefield Commission responsible for the placement of monuments on the battlefield. While engaged in the work and while at this spot, Gen. Fullerton mentioned the daring of the Confederate color-bearer, unknown to him, as he saw it in the battle and said, "It was the bravest act that I witnessed during the war."

The Federal defensive line from here all the way to the right over Hill 2 was held by the brigade of 40-year-old Ohioan Col. Ferdinand Van Derveer. Van Derveer's brigade was a part of Gen. John Brannan's division, and arguably might have had the best combat record of any brigade on either side that fought at Chickamauga – saving the Army of the Cumberland no fewer than six times during the two-day battle.

Colonel Ferdinand Van Derveer, USA   His brigade had the most distinguished combat record of any brigade that fought at Chickamauga

At the time of Longstreet's breakthrough at the Brotherton house, Van Derveer's brigade was reforming and resting in the north Kelly Field, where they had just finished repulsing the charge of Maj. Gen. John C. Breckenridge's division. At 2:00 p.m., hearing heavy firing to his right-rear and learning that Gen. Brannan held the high ground (Hill 1) with the remnants of his division, Van Derveer decided to join them. He moved cautiously through the woods and reported to Thomas around 2:30 p.m. "Glad to see you, Colonel," said Thomas. "What condition is your brigade in?" Van Derveer answered, "All in line, save our dead and wounded." Van Derveer was directed to assume this line centered on the top of Hill 2: the 9th Ohio on the left, followed by the 87th Indiana, 2nd Minnesota, and 35th Ohio in that order.

The 9th Ohio was an all-German unit. In this regiment, all orders were given in German, and their commander, the tough and profane Col. Gustav Kammerling, had a propensity for bayonet charges. As soon as the 9th arrived in line, to the amazement of the units to their left, Col. Kammerling ordered them over the crest of the ridge in a bayonet charge—their second of the day (and third of the battle, so far). As soon as the 9th was out of sight down the slope, there was a crash of musketry, followed by the regiment returning quickly to their place in the line. "Dem got dam rebels are too thick down there [sic]," snarled the unrepentant colonel. Late in the afternoon, and out of ammunition, Kammerling would lead the 9th Ohio in a successful bayonet charge, clearing the slopes of Confederates and relieving the pressure on this part of the line. This charge is depicted in the diorama in the Visitor Center.

9th Ohio Infantry.
This all-German regiment, under the command of Colonel Gustave Kammerling, had a propensity for bayonet charges. The diorama in the Visitor Center depicts one of their charges down Snodgrass Hill.

The hard-fighting 2nd Minnesota had a unique claim after the Battle of Chickamauga: not one man in the regiment was a straggler nor had any been captured. The 2nd Minnesota had entered the battle with 384 men and had 222 men answer the roll afterwards. All the rest were known casualties. An officer of the 2nd Minnesota, J.W. Bishop, said of the action here: "Again the order was passed to aim carefully and make every shot count, and the deadly work began. The front ranks melted away under the rapid fire of our men, those following bowed their heads to the storm of bullets and pressed on, some of them falling at every step, until, the supporting touch of elbows being lost, the survivors hesitate, halt, and then turning, start back with a rush that carries away to the rear all that escape the bullets, as deadly in the wild retreat as in the desperate and orderly advance. This was all repeated again and again, until the slope was so covered with dead and wounded men that, looking from our position, we could hardly see the ground. Never was any position more gallantly assaulted or more desperately defended."

Sgt. Axel Reed of the 2nd Minnesota was under arrest as the battle began. He had insulted an officer over the quality of food when the men had been given wormy hardtack to eat. He and a comrade left camp (with a pass, he claimed) to go look for blackberries. The officer took offense at Reed's criticism and leave-taking, and now as the battle raged, Sgt. Reed was under guard behind the lines. Reed was furious. He yelled at the private guarding him to let him go to the fight. He berated the private so long and so loudly that the poor soldier relented. Unarmed, Sgt. Reed ran to the battle line where he picked up a rifle and fought with a heroism that stood out even amongst all the courageous acts committed that day.

Sergeant Axel Reed of the 2nd Minnesota. This photograph was made in 1865 when Reed was a lieutenant.

For his actions here during the battle, Sgt. Axel Reed was awarded one of the nine Medals of Honor given at Chickamauga. (Sgt. Reed also fought courageously during the 2nd Minnesota's charge up Missionary Ridge on November 25, 1863, losing an arm in that battle. Despite the loss of an arm, he remained in the Army, being discharged at the end of the war as a first Lieutenant.)

Van Derveer's brigade bridged the area between Hill 1 and the 21st Ohio. They were able to relieve some of Brannan's tired troops who retired 200 yards to rest and replenish ammunition—a constant problem on Horseshoe Ridge that day. They held the line all afternoon against the incessant Confederate attacks. Van Derveer recalled, "For an hour and a half before dark the attack was one of unexampled fury, line after line of fresh troops being hurled against our position with a heroism and persistency which almost distinguished their cause." Captain Fredrick Keil, commanding Company C of the 35th Ohio, simply stated, "The struggle was that of sheer desperation." VanDerveer's brigade lost 50 percent of its men at Chickamauga.

Directions: Turn left; keep bearing right along the crest of Hill 1 for 100 yards. At the peak of the hill, you will come to the large monument to the 82nd Indiana of   Connell's brigade. Stand at the peak of Hill 1. Along the way you will see monuments to the 87th Indiana and 9th Ohio of Van Derveer's brigade. Also here are many monuments and tablets to the various commands that drifted to this hill to defend it. Feel free to view them.

Dedication of the Chickamauga and Chattanooga National Military Park

An early view of the 2nd Minnesota Monument, ca. 1895.

MAP 8

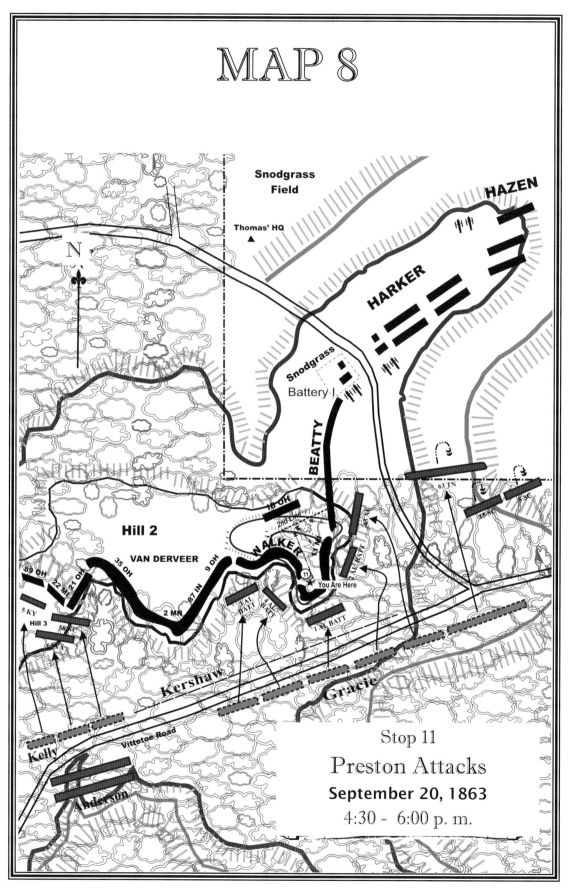

Snodgrass
Field

HAZEN

Thomas' HQ

N

HARKER

Snodgrass
Battery I

BEATTY

63 TN

Hill 2

15 OH

2nd Line

VAN DERVEER

WALKER

89 OH

22 MI

21 OH

35 OH

9 OH

You Are Here

11

5 KY

Hill 3

58 NC

2 MN

87 IN

3 AL BATU

4 AL BATU

1 AL BATT

Kershaw

Gracie

Kelly

Vittetoe Road

Stop 11

Preston Attacks

September 20, 1863

4:30 - 6:00 p.m.

Anderson

STOP 11 - A

Hill 1: A Time for Leadership

When James Longstreet's brigades pierced the Federal line at the Brotherton house, he shattered the Union right and center. The Federal divisions of Davis and Sheridan (along with Army of the Cumberland commander Rosecrans and two of his three corps commanders) were driven westward and off the battlefield. Broken regiments and fragments of units from divisions belonging to Wood, Negley, Van Cleve, and Brannan were driven northwestward and began to rally here on the hills around the Snodgrass farm.

Federal division commander Gen. John Brannan arrived at noon with the survivors of Croxton's and Connell's brigades. Brannan quickly began to organize a defense along the ridge crest, taking advantage of this, the highest ground on the battlefield. Fragments of regiments and companies, even individual soldiers, were rallied and placed into the line. Col. Moses Walker, even though under arrest for some minor infraction and serving without a command, greatly aided Brannan in placing these fragments into a line of battle. Brannan realized the value of an officer as excellent as Walker, released him from arrest, and placed him in command of all the units on Hill 1. Brig. Gen. John Beatty arrived on the hill with the remnants of his brigade. Unwilling to leave the battlefield after his brigade had been almost destroyed by Gen.

Brigadier General John M. Brannan, USA. Brannan played a pivotal role in the defense of Snodgrass Hill.

John C. Breckenridge's Confederate division and driven westward, Beatty extended a line that ran from Brannan's left flank down the hill to the Snodgrass house.

General John Beatty's line ran from Brannan's left flank to the Snodgrass House.

But mostly it was the *men* who decided to fight. The Union infantry who gathered here were tough Westerners with plenty of fight left in them. Natural leaders, not all of them officers, called on the men retreating to turn and fight. Soldiers stopped to fight with a unit not their own because of the entreaties of a tough sergeant or corporal to "rally 'round the flag." In the valuable hour that Col. Charles Harker's brigade bought for the Army of the Cumberland out in the Dyer field (Stop 2), a make-shift line of battle formed on the crest of Hill 1. Eventually Harker's brigade came out of the woods after its fight with Kershaw's Confederates and extended the Federal left. The 21st Ohio moved up Hill 2 and extended the Union right, making a battle line about a half-mile in length. As quickly as possible, men gathered logs, fence rails, rocks, limbs, and any other material that could stop a bullet and formed a low crude breastwork. By 12:45 p.m., Brannan had some 3,400 men—Harker's brigade, the 21st Ohio infantry regiment, Battery I of the 4th U.S. Artillery, and remnants of various commands—in line on a one-half mile front ready to receive the Southerners.

As they formed their line of battle here on Hill 1, the officers and men of these various Federal units felt intense apprehension. Up to this time, the Confederates had overwhelmed the right half of the Union army. Most of the men standing on this hill had been over-run or forced to retreat. Could they hold against the supposed thousands of Confederates that were about to emerge from the forest below them? Would they be outflanked and overwhelmed as well? Would the man or unit next to them stand fast and weather the storm of bullets, bayonets, and shells? All this was unknown as they quickly formed their lines on this hill.

Brannan's first defense line was rallied here.

Gen. John Beatty remembered after the Civil War: "I found abundant opportunity to make myself useful. Gathering up scattered attachments of a dozen different commands, I filled up an unoccupied space on the ridge between Harker, of Wood's division, on the left, and Brannan, on the right, and this point we held obstinately until sunset. Colonel Stoughton, Eleventh Michigan; Lieutenant-Colonel Rappin, Nineteenth Illinois; Lieutenant-Colonel Grosvenor, Eighteenth Ohio; Colonel Hunter, Eightysecond Indiana; Colonel Hays and Lieutenant-Colonel Wharton, Tenth Kentucky; Captain Stinchcomb, Seventeenth Ohio; and Captain Kendrick, Seventy-ninth Pennsylvania, were there, each having a few men of their respective commands."

Brigadier General John Beatty, USA

No sooner had the line formed than Kershaw's South Carolinians ascended Horseshoe Ridge at 1:15 p.m. (Map 3, page 34). In Kershaw's view, all he had to do was push the Federals and they would break. But during the pursuit, Kershaw's regiments had become separated and somewhat broken. The first attack here on Hill 1 was made by the 7th and 15th South Carolina, which were surprised by the solid Union defense. After receiving several volleys of well-directed fire from the ridge crest, Kershaw's men withdrew back to the Vittetoe Road to regroup.

With the quick repulse of Kershaw's first attack, the Federal soldiers gained confidence in their ability to hold this high ground. It was a good defensive position, and now, to the blue infantry, the Confederates did not seem quite so invincible. In addition, shortly after the repulse of Kershaw, Gen. George H. Thomas rode down the battle line, inspiring confidence in the officers and men. Thomas meant to hold, and he communicated that determination to all who saw and heard him.

Kershaw made three determined attacks on Hill 1, the last at 2:30 p.m. The attacks exhibited great courage and savagery, with the men at times fighting face-to-face across the low breastwork. Gen. Brannan wrote, "Nothing can exceed the desperate determination with which the rebels endeavored to gain possession of this point, hurling entire divisions on my small force in their fierce eagerness to obtain a position which would undoubtedly have given them the grand advantage of the day. My troops maintained their ground with obstinacy, evincing great gallantry and devotion in the most trying circumstances. I remained in this position, heavily engaged, until sunset."

Gen. John Beatty continued: "…and they [the Union officers] and their men fought and struggled and clung to that ridge with an obstinate, persistent, desperate courage, unsurpassed, I believe, on any field. I robbed the dead of cartridges and distributed them to the men; and once when, after a desperate struggle, our troops were driven from the crest, and the enemy's flag waved above it, the men were rallied, and I rode up the hill with them, waving my hat, and shouting like a madman. Thus we charged, and the enemy only saved his colors by throwing them down the hill. However much we may say of those who held command, justice compels the acknowledgment that no officer exhibited more courage on that occasion than the humblest private in the ranks."

In the interval between attacks, the men on the hill and the Southerners down on the Vittetoe Road kept up heavy skirmishing. The firing never ceased, but after Kershaw's last attack was driven off about 3:00 p.m., a relative lull came over this part of the line. Steedman had arrived at 2:00 p.m. and the fight had extended to the Union right as the Southerners attempted to flank the Federal defenses there. The Union defenders could hear the roar of battle off to their right.

<u>Note:</u> You may want to view the monument to the 7th South Carolina regiment, down the trail 40 yards, directly in front of the 82nd Indiana monument.

<u>Directions:</u> Turn to your left and proceed 50 yards down the Federal line to the monument that has the statue of a Union officer on the top. This is the monument to the 11th Michigan Infantry. The officer on top of the monument is Col. William L. Stoughton. Turn right and face down the hill.

Michigan at Chickamauga

**Early visitors to the Chickamauga Battlefield
view the newly dedicated monuments on Hill 1, ca. 1895**

Harker's line as seen from Hill 1

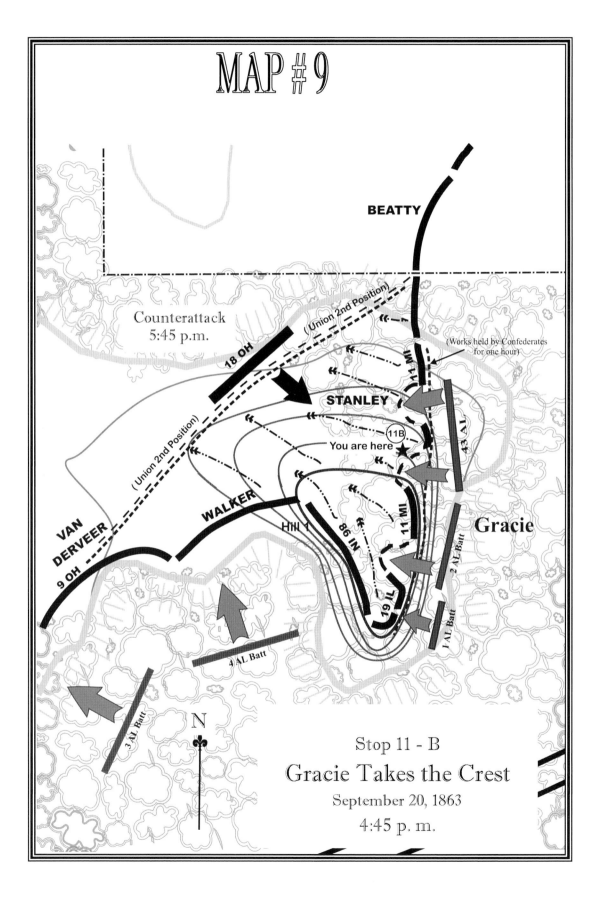

MAP #9

BEATTY

Counterattack
5:45 p.m.

(Union 2nd Position)

18 OH

(Works held by Confederates
for one hour)

11 MI

STANLEY

43 AL

11B

You are here

(Union 2nd Position)

WALKER

Gracie

VAN
DERVEER

Hill 1

11 MI

86 IN

2 AL Batt

9 OH

19 IL

1 AL Batt

4 AL Batt

3 AL Batt

N

Stop 11 - B

Gracie Takes the Crest

September 20, 1863

4:45 p. m.

STOP 11 - B

A relative lull in the battle was about to end violently for the Union troops on Hill 1. Confederate Brigadier General William Preston's three-brigade division moved rapidly forward. At 4:30 p.m., Col. John Kelly's brigade attacked Hill 3 (Stop 8) and Brig. Gen. Archibald Gracie, Jr.'s 2,003-man brigade assaulted Hill 1. Mostly consisting of Alabama troops, Gracie's brigade had never been in a large battle before.

Gracie, 30 years old at Chickamauga, was from New York City. His father was a wealthy merchant there (Gracie Mansion is now the official residence of the mayor of New York City). In 1856, Gracie, a West Point graduate, resigned from the army and moved to Mobile, Alabama, to

Chickamauga Battlefield Park

The 11th Michigan Monument on Hill 1 in an early view

enter business with his father. That same year he took a Southern bride. Archibald Gracie, Jr. would fight for the South.

Gracie's brigade consisted of the 1st, 2nd, 3rd, and 4th Alabama battalions (collectively called Hilliard's Legion) plus the 43rd Alabama and 63rd Tennessee regiments. After Gracie deployed in line of battle behind Kershaw's brigade around 4:15 p.m., Kershaw suddenly and prematurely ordered Gracie to the attack without Preston's knowledge. Kershaw promised Gracie support on the left by the 2nd South Carolina and on the

New York born Brigadier General Archibald Gracie, Jr., CSA

right by the 15th and 8th South Carolina from his command. At 4:30 p.m., the Southern infantry swept across the Vittetoe Road and up the hill. The historian of the 1st Alabama Battalion wrote, "The first volley of the enemy, who were lying in wait behind a fortification of logs in an excellent position, bore with fatal precision upon our line, and created many a gap in our heretofore intact ranks; but it was responded to by an answering volley and a rousing cheer, which rose high above the din of conflict. I shall attempt no recital of what followed—the heart grows sick at the memory."

Young Henry Haynie, 19th Illinois, witnessed the charge of the 1st Alabama Battalion from the top of the ridge: "Again the foe comes on in renewed assault; they come so swiftly that we can hardly count their volleying. … Through the thick smoke suddenly we see a swarm of men in gray, not in battle-line, but an on-coming mass of soldiers bent on burying bullets in resisting flesh."

The 11th Michigan took the brunt of the 2nd Alabama Battalion's violent attack. Col. William Stoughton recalled, "A contest ensued, which in its fierceness and duration has few parallels. The enemy was in heavy force, and fought with the most determined obstinacy. As fast as their ranks were thinned by our fire they were filled up by fresh troops. A dense cloud of smoke enveloped our lines, and in some places the position of the foe could only be known by the flash of his guns." Another member of the 11th Michigan stated,

Defense line on Hill 1. Artillery is one section (two cannons) of Battery 1, 4th U.S.

"The slope in our front was strewn with the enemy's dead, so thick you could almost walk on them, our men's faces were black with powder smoke, their tongues fairly hung out for want of water."

Along the front of the 11th Michigan the fighting was hand-to-hand. Men fought savagely with the bayonet. They clubbed skulls with the butts of their rifles. At the breastworks, the commander of the 2nd Alabama

Battalion, Lt. Col. Bolling Hall, Jr., was severely wounded and the color-bearer was hit three times and the flag staff shot away. Still the men charged ahead. The Hilliard Legion flag reportedly had 83 bullet holes in it after the battle.

Witnessing the attack, Kershaw wrote afterwards, "This was one of the heaviest attacks of the war on a single point."

Federal troops here on the crest could not withstand pressure from so many fresh troops and began to give way. The Federals in this sector retreated back 100 yards to the northern slope of Hill 1 (behind you, across from the modern park road), where they held. The Confederates, severe casualties greatly reducing their numbers, could not advance farther than the Union breastworks, however. The 1st, 2nd, and 3rd Alabama Battalions, plus the 43rd Alabama, held the hillcrest hoping for reinforcements and ammunition, neither of which appeared. The two sides fired at each other through the smoke across the hilltop.

For an hour, Gracie's men held the abandoned Federal works. Then they began to run out of ammunition. Beatty and Stoughton noticed the reduced rate of fire. Perceiving the Southerners to be low on ammunition, they ordered the 18th Ohio, who had been kept in reserve, to counterattack and retake the works. Just as the 18th Ohio charged with fixed bayonets the Confederates fired their last volley. Gracie ordered the exhausted Southern infantry off the hill.

The 18th Ohio Infantry counter-attacked Gracie's men on the crest of Hill 1 at 5:45 p. m. The attack moved from right to left in this view. The 18th Ohio Monument is just left of center.

18th Ohio Monument

A Union veteran recalled that as Stoughton's men resumed their places on the line, some soldiers began singing the "Battle Cry of Freedom." Soon, all the Federal soldiers were singing it at the top of their voices, "and when they came to the words 'Down with the traitors, up with the Stars,' every fellow emphasized them with a vim that made the woods and rocky hills sing."

As an indicator of the savage fighting during Gracie's attack, his brigade of 2,003 officers and men took 725 casualties—more than a third of his brigade—in only 90 minutes of combat.

 <u>Directions:</u> **After viewing the monuments in this area, walk northeast down the park road 220 yards to the Snodgrass house. Stand anywhere convenient in front of the house.**

STOP 12 - A

The Snodgrass House
and
The Rock of Chickamauga

Stop 12 - A
The George Washington Snodgrass House

Snodgrass Hill takes its name from the family who owned this land and farmed these fields in September 1863. George Washington Snodgrass moved from Virginia to the Chattanooga area sometime before 1843. The deed for the purchase of this farm was recorded on September 8, 1855. George Snodgrass, a carpenter as well as a farmer, lived here with his third wife, Elizabeth, and their seven children. One son, John, was a private in the Army of Tennessee.

At the time of the Battle of Chickamauga, the house that stood here was of a "dogtrot" design: two structures connected by a covered breezeway. Behind the main house stood a smokehouse and a small servants' quarters. Across the lane was a barn. A split-rail fence surrounded the house and smokehouse. A peach orchard grew to the west of the house, and a large cornfield ran across the open ridge spur north and northeast of the farm compound (Stop 13).

Dedication of the Chickamauga and Chattanooga National Military Park

The Snodgrass House—an early view

The house you see here is not the original Snodgrass house. By 1900, the original house was in a dilapidated condition and was torn down and replaced by the replica you see here. It is very likely that the present structure contains logs from the original house. Unfortunately, the barn and smokehouse were also torn down by the Park Service in the 1950s.

During and after the battle the buildings of the Snodgrass farm were used to shelter the many wounded from the surrounding fight. As the floor space in these structures filled up, the wounded (mostly Union soldiers) lay unprotected in the Snodgrass yard. A hospital was set up here to treat as many casualties as possible.

George Snodgrass was determined to stay in the house with his family during the battle, but when bullets and shell fragments began to penetrate the roof of his house on September 19, he and his family fled north. They camped out in a ravine with some of the other local families until the battle was over. Upon returning, they found the house, as a daughter later wrote, "a gory shambles." The family moved once again and did not return for more than a year. Attempting to resume their quiet life, they found they could no longer farm the fields or harvest the lumber on their land. The huge amount of lead and iron in the ground and in the trees from bullets and shot ruined plows and saws, making their farm virtually unusable.

Chickamauga Battlefield Park

Then and Now
The Snodgrass House

 **Directions:** The artillery you see in the front yard of the Snodgrass house is from Battery I, 4th U.S. Artillery. Cross Snodgrass Lane and walk to the last (fourth) cannon. Stop and face left, looking down the reverse (north) slope of Snodgrass Hill.

Dedication of the Chickamauga and Chattanooga National Military Park

Early photograph of the scene of Kershaw's and Gracie's attacks up Snodgrass Hill. The park road exists today.

STOP 12 - B

Stop 12 - B
Thomas' headquarters at the foot of Snodgrass Hill.
Note the cannons to Battery 1, 4th U.S., on the crest of the hill.

The small pyramid of cannonballs you see about 200 yards down the hill marks the spot of the field headquarters for Major General George H. Thomas. From this area, Thomas directed the defense of Snodgrass Hill and Horseshoe Ridge, spending time receiving reports and giving orders. Having to fight a battle in two sectors simultaneously, his attention was equally divided between the defense of Horseshoe Ridge and his other four divisions in place around the Kelly farm. Thomas would occasionally ride the battle line, making suggestions and inspiring the men by his solid presence. Captain Horace C. Long, who fought on Horseshoe Ridge with the 87th Indiana of van Derveer's Brigade, wrote in a letter dated October 21, 1863: "General Thomas was here in person encouraging the men and telling them to hold out, for everything depended upon holding the ridge. When it seemed that we could not stand the shot and shell that were hurled at us in such showers and were about to give way, all the officers pitched in promiscuously to cheering and encouraging the men of all regiments alike. General Thomas would jump off his horse, swing his hat, rush among the men and encourage them by his own acts of valor."

At 3:35 p.m., Rosecrans' chief of staff, Brigadier General James A. Garfield (future President of the United States), reached Thomas with the first reliable report of the defeat of the Federal right flank and news that Rosecrans was in Chattanooga. Garfield wrote, "I shall never forget my amazement and admiration when I beheld Thomas holding his own with utter defeat on each side and wild confusion in the rear."

At 4:15 p.m., Rosecrans, unaware of the stand being made on Horseshoe Ridge, sent Thomas a message ordering him to retreat to Rossville. Even after stating to Garfield, "It will ruin the army to withdraw it now," Thomas, his men exhausted and almost out of ammunition, knew he had to retreat eventually. He appointed Granger to supervise the withdrawal of the Horseshoe Ridge line. Thomas would begin the phased retreat of his two fronts beginning with the withdrawal of the Kelly field line, followed by the Horseshoe Ridge sector. With these instructions given, Thomas and his staff rode to the Kelly field to direct the withdrawal of his four divisions there.

Garfield, in a message sent to Rosecrans in Chattanooga, stated, "Thomas is standing like a rock." Assistant Secretary of War Charles Dana, present at the battle, wired Washington from Chattanooga that evening, "Our troops were as immovable as the rocks they stood on. … Thomas seemed to have filled every soldier with his own unconquerable firmness." With "everything gone but manhood and the ground they stood on," as one eyewitness said, Gen. George H. Thomas had saved the Army of the Cumberland from disaster.

"There is nothing finer in history than Thomas at Chickamauga," wrote military historian General Henry M. Cist. George Henry Thomas was born in Southampton County, Virginia, on July 31, 1816. He attended West Point , graduating twelfth in the Class of 1840. Thomas served in the Seminole and Mexican wars and served as a major in the pre-war 2nd U.S. Cavalry regiment, in which fellow Virginian Robert E. Lee was lieutenant colonel and Albert Sidney Johnston (killed at Shiloh) was colonel.

When the country split in two in 1861, Thomas remained loyal to the United States. His two sisters in Virginia turned his picture to the wall and never spoke to him again. When they were informed of his death in 1870, one of them remarked, "Our brother George died to us in 1861."

In December of 1862, in the debacle of the first day at the Battle of Stones River when the right wing of the Army of the

Major General George H. Thomas
"The Rock of Chickamauga"

Cumberland shattered, Thomas' corps had held firm and beaten back Bragg's attacks. George Thomas was a consummate professional and kept his cool in the noise and confusion of combat. He was personally fearless, stating, "I don't see how a man can be an infidel and remain a brave man. Belief in God is like confidence in one's General, it holds us to the front."

Perhaps one of the greatest tributes to Thomas at Chickamauga was given by one of his generals: the hatless, bloodied, "spell my name right" General James Steedman. When once asked why Thomas was able to hold on while other corps commanders failed, Steedman said, "I'll tell you. Such was the awe and veneration in which he was held that not one of his men dared leave his post. When they were in live fighting, they knew the old man was on deck, and they would rather have died than go to the rear, unless they were carried. Death was preferable to letting General Thomas see them retreating. I had the same feeling myself. I would have died before appearing to Thomas to be doing anything but my whole duty, and I would have felt myself forever disgraced."

Gen. George H. Thomas was forever known as "The Rock of Chickamauga." He died of a stroke in his office while on duty in San Francisco on March 28, 1870. He never returned to his home in Southampton County. The only statue to General Thomas sits in Thomas Circle in Washington, D.C. He looks south, toward his native Virginia.

Thomas Statue, Washington, DC

Directions: Turn to your right and walk 140 yards down the line of monuments to Harker's and Hazen's Federal brigades until you reach the monument with the tiger on top. This is the monument to the 125th Ohio, "Opdycke's Tigers." Stand beside the monument and face in the direction the tiger is facing—east, down the hill.

STOP - 13

Harker Hill
"We will hold it or die here."

Stop 13
Harker's line, looking northeast.

Between 12:45 p.m. and 1:00 p.m., Col. Charles Harker's Federal brigade moved out of the woods to your front and began to form a line of battle across this hill. They had been driven out of the Dyer field by Kershaw's Confederate brigade (Stop 2), and now they were looking for a good position on which to rally. They knew the Confederates were right behind them and would attack them again at any moment.

In their repulse of Robertson's Texas brigade, and in their brief stand against Kershaw's South Carolina brigade, Harker had bought a valuable hour of time in which retreating Union troops could be halted and formed on the high ground of Hill 1. Without this gift of one hour, the scattered Federal units likely could not have maintained their hold on Horseshoe Ridge. Now Harker, along with a few fragments of other commands, formed his line across this hill in the Snodgrass cornfield. His men would be the left flank of the Union defenses in this sector. Some 1,200 men were now ready to receive the Confederate attack along the Snodgrass spur.

Moments after they had formed their line, they saw the Confederates, the 8th South Carolina of Kershaw's brigade, advancing through the trees. Heavy fire from Harker's brigade plus blasts of canister from Battery I, 4th U.S. Artillery halted the Confederates at the edge of the woods. The South Carolinians lay down and fired toward the Union line on the hill.

As the roar of this attack continued, Thomas rode up to Harker. "This hill must be held and I trust you to do it," he said to Harker. Harker replied, "We will hold it or die here." Satisfied, Thomas rode over to Col. Emerson Opdycke, commander of the 125th Ohio, the newly christened "Opdycke's Tigers." "You must hold this position at all hazards," he commanded. "We will hold this ground or go to Heaven from it," answered Opdycke.

Colonel Emerson Opdycke, USA. The 125th Ohio became known as "Opdycke's Tigers" after the battle.

Since this position was in a cornfield with no readily available material for breastworks, Harker, a sound battlefield tactician, used the crest of this spur to protect his men. Forming his brigade in two lines, he ordered the first line to the hilltop to fire their volley, after which they would move back a few paces to reload, completely protected from enemy fire by the hillcrest as the second line moved up to fire. Roland Crutchfield of the 65th Ohio, Harker's Brigade, wrote in 1909: "The Rebs came on to us and the ball opened in earnest. We were formed in two lines when the first line give [sic] them a volley it fell back and second line would take its place. The fighting that long afternoon was all done in open or cleaned ground."

A bronze bas relief on the 65th Ohio Monument depicting combat on "Harker's Hill."

These highly effective tactics drove Major John Stackhouse of the 8th

South Carolina into a fury. Stackhouse was, by all accounts, "a pure Christian gentleman and churchman of the purest sect." No one could remember his ever using profane language in camp or battle. "He was always sincere and his language chosen and chaste." That is, until he was pinned down in this cornfield by the devastating volleys of Harker's brigade. When Harker's men would appear on the crest, Stackhouse would yell, "There they are boys! Give them hell!" And then he would mutter to himself, "May God forgive me for that." Before his men could fire,

Looking down and across the Snodgrass cornfield from behind the 125th Ohio line. Harker's brigade used the hill crest as a natural breastwork to protect their men.

the Federals moved back out of sight. Again the Federals appeared. "Boys, give it to them, give them hell!" But Harker's men again moved back out of sight. Frustrated beyond reason, he lost his temper. Standing up in the cornfield, the pious Stackhouse yelled at the top of his voice, "Give them hell! Give them hell! I tell you boys, give them hell! God *damn* their souls!"

At 1:30 p.m., Confederate Brigadier General Benjamin Humphreys pushed his Mississippi brigade to the bottom of the hill but failed to make the expected attack. Humphreys had assumed command of the brigade after Brigadier General William Barksdale was mortally wounded at Gettysburg. Humphreys was not the aggressive commander Barksdale had been. When he caught sight of the Federal troops and artillery on the crest of the hill, he halted his brigade. For several minutes while he decided what to do, his brigade stood in a crossfire, needlessly losing 152 killed and wounded. He decided that to attack would cost "half his brigade," so he withdrew back to the north end of the Dyer field. His excellent brigade would take no further part in the battle. One of the "what ifs" of the Battle of Chickamauga is what might have happened had Longstreet ordered Humphreys' Mississippi, Benning's Georgia, Sheffield's Alabama, and Robertson's Texas brigades from the Army of Northern Virginia into that half-mile gap between the Snodgrass Hill-Horseshoe Ridge line and the four divisions holding the ridge east of the Kelly farm.

During the day, this part of the Union line received reinforcements. Around 2:30 p.m., the 18th Ohio Battery from Steedman's division arrived on Harker's left flank, their 3-inch ordnance rifles giving much needed artillery support to that end of the line. In addition, at 5:30 p.m. Brigadier General William B. Hazen's brigade from Palmer's division arrived, but not before Harker had stopped the most determined charge of the day.

Dedication of the Chickamauga and Chattanooga National Military Park

**An early view of Harker's line.
Note the Snodgrass barn in the background.**

Shortly before 4:30 p.m., Archibald Gracie's Alabama brigade attacked on a wide front (Map 8, page 86). In front of Harker, the 63rd Tennessee from Gracie's brigade, supported by the 8th and 15th South Carolina from Kershaw's brigade, attacked into the cornfield. The 63rd Tennessee took heavy casualties from Harker's well-timed volleys, which pinned down all three regiments. After a full hour of firing, and running out of ammunition, the Confederates broke off the uneven contest and withdrew back across the Vittetoe Road. The 63rd Tennessee had lost 200 men out of the 400 they had brought into the fight. Harker's brigade hardly lost a man.

Harker held this hill until ordered to withdraw to Rossville after darkness had fallen on the battlefield. Col. Charles Harker was promoted to Brigadier General on April 10, 1864, shortly before the beginning of the Atlanta Campaign. He was killed at Cheatham Hill during the Battle of Kennesaw Mountain, June 27, 1864.

Modern view of Harker's line.

Directions: After viewing the monuments in this area (please take time to view the bronze bas reliefs on some of them), return to the park road and turn left, descending the hill. On your way down the road, notice the stone marker to the 63rd Tennessee, just to the left of the road. A few yards farther to the left you will see the stone marker for the 8th South Carolina. To the right, as you descend the hill, sharp eyes will see the stone marker for the 15th South Carolina, about half way up Hill 1.

Turn right at the fork in the park road onto the Vittetoe Road and stop in front of the tablet for Gracie's brigade. Face in the direction of the tablet looking up the hill.

Gracie's Brigade attacked Hill 1 at this point, holding the hillcrest for one hour.

The monument for the 63rd Tennessee of Gracie's brigade. This regiment incurred 200 casualties out of the 400 men that attacked Harker's line—a staggering casualty rate of 50%. The marker to the 8th South Carolina of Kershaw's brigade is visible in the background.

STOP 14

The Cost of the Battle
"and naught remained of all the glory"

The Battle of Chickamauga was a bloodletting. In two days of furious combat, more than 37,000 Americans had been killed, wounded, captured or listed as missing. While one can find variations in the final statistics, Chickamauga National Military Park has the number of casualties listed as follows:

	Union	Confederate
Killed	1,656	2,673
Wounded	9,749	16,274
Missing	4,774	2,003
Total	16,179	20,950

Chickamauga was one of those rare battles in the Civil War in which the Confederate army outnumbered the Union army (Confederate—66,000 engaged; Union—58,000 engaged). The Confederates were almost always on the attack during the battle, making their losses higher than those of the Union army.

Approximately 14,700 Confederates fought 10,000 Federals for control of Horseshoe Ridge. During the six hours of fighting between 1:00 p.m. and 7:00 p.m., the Confederates launched fully sixteen brigade-sized attacks against the Union defenses. To the Northerners the attacks seemed continuous. Because of incomplete and missing after-action reports, reliable casualty figures for the action here are impossible to compute, but the losses were high. According to the tablets on the battlefield, Preston's division lost 32.71 percent of its men on Horseshoe Ridge; Kershaw's brigade lost 33 percent; Gracie's brigade lost 36.2 percent in 90 minutes; Anderson's brigade lost 29.91 percent. Other units had similar losses.

Fighting behind make-shift breastworks and not having to charge up the steep slope, the Union casualties were much lower but still significant. The closeness of the combatants and the persistent attacks made for lethal fighting, which was hand-to-hand at times. Both sides fought with a courage and devotion to duty seldom seen on any battlefield of the Civil War.

After Chickamauga, Archibald Gracie, Jr., had just over a year to live. He was killed instantly by an exploding artillery shell on December 2, 1864, in the Petersburg, Virginia trenches. Gen. Gracie's son, Archibald Gracie IV, was five years old at the time of his father's death. In later life, hearing tales of his father's bravery from veterans and learning of the many inaccuracies in the history of the Battle of Chickamauga, Gracie spent seven years writing *The Truth About Chickamauga*. Following its publication in 1912, Gracie decided to relax and took passage to Europe on board the *Oceanic*. He booked his return trip on a new ship making its maiden voyage, the *Titanic*. He departed from Southampton traveling in first class. Gracie survived the sinking of the *Titanic*, being one of the last people to leave the ship. Gracie never fully recovered from exposure in the frigid water. He was the third to die of those who were rescued, passing away on December 4, 1912, while editing his latest book: *The Truth About the Titanic*.

After the fighting had died down on that bloody September Sunday night, an unidentified Southern newspaper correspondent described the scenes he had witnessed. He wrote: "The groups of dead men and horses, and writhing forms of the wounded, there in that dreary forest, only seen by the scattered moonbeams as they stole through the branches, and the flickering firelight, as it crept slowly but steadily up to where they lay, and the fearful cries of those who watched its advance, unable to drag their broken limbs beyond the reach of the destroyer: and then the distorted and upturned faces of those whose bodies were lying amidst the grim shadows which fell around, conspicuous among which was the shadow of death. All the pompous pageantry of the scene was gone, and naught remained of all the glory lost and won upon that bloody field save the wretched forms of those who no more will spring forward at the call of arms."

Directions: **The tour is completed. You will have noticed your car parked immediately behind you. I sincerely hope you have enjoyed your walking tour of Horseshoe Ridge and that you have a renewed appreciation for the Americans who gave their all fighting for this rocky hill.**

Suggested Reading List

Many of these titles can be found in the Visitor Center Bookstore.

This Terrible Sound, The Battle of Chickamauga
by Peter Cozzens (1992)

The Maps of Chickamauga
by David A. Powell (2009)

The Chickamauga Campaign
Edited by Steven E. Woodworth (2010)

A Deep Steady Thunder
by Steven E. Woodworth (1998)

Chickamauga, Bloody Battle in the West
by Glenn Tucker (1961)

The U. S. Army War College Guide to the Battle of Chickamauga by Matt Spruill (1993)

Six Armies in Tennessee, The Chickamauga and Chattanooga Campaigns by Steven E. Woodworth (1998)

Blue and Gray Magazine:

Fall 2006, The Fall of Chattanooga. By William Glenn Robertson
Spring 2007, Bragg's Lost Opportunity. By William Glenn Robertson
Fall 2007, The Armies Collide! By William Glenn Robertson
Spring 2008, Chickamauga Day 1. By William Glenn Robertson
Summer 2008, Chickamauga, September 20, 1863.
By William Glenn Robertson

About The Author

Robert L. Carter is an educator with 38 years experience teaching high school in Georgia, Virginia and Alabama. Raised in Chatsworth, Georgia, a town close to the battlefield, he graduated with Bachelor of Science and Masters Degrees from Jacksonville State University in Alabama.

His father first introduced him to the Chickamauga Battlefield when he was six years old. Since that time, Mr. Carter has been a serious student of Civil War history.

Robert Carter's passion for, and intricate knowledge of Civil War history shines in *The Fight for Snodgrass Hill and the Rock of Chickamauga.* This walking tour guide transports the reader into the full fledged battle where gallant men fought with honor to victory or death.

He is a frequent lecturer and tour guide, and is currently working on the second walking tour guide book in this series.

Bronze bas relief from the 22nd Michigan Monument on Hill 3